Pat Doran's
Phonics Steps to Reading Success

*A Fast-Paced, Word-Attack System
For Developing & Improving
Reading and Spelling Skills*

_____ 5th Edition _____

Easy to teach. Easy to learn.

For all ages: children, youth, adult

Phonics skills to read and spell correctly.

www.edu-steps.com

Pat Doran's
Phonics Steps to Reading Success

*A Fast-Paced, Word-Attack System
For Developing & Improving
Reading Skills*

5th Edition

Pat Doran, M.Ed.

with Lisa Cragg and Joy Doran

Copyright © 2015 Pat Doran, M.Ed.
Published by Edu-Steps, Inc. Phoenix, Arizona

ISBN: 978-0-9771101-8-6

Please respect the intellectual property of the author or Edu-Steps, Inc.
No part of this book may be used or reproduced in any manner whatsoever without written permission from the author or publisher, except noted in the program, or in the case of brief quotations, embodied in critical articles and reviews.

☆ Special Note of Appreciation ☆ *Thank you to JEANNIE ELLER of Action Reading for her dedication, enthusiasm, and inspiration. Some ideas, organization, and linguistic design of Phonics Steps to Reading Success were inspired by George O. Cureton, Action Reading, the Participatory Approach, Allyn and Bacon, Inc., Boston, 1973.* www.actionreading.com.

Dedicated to
S. Naomi Kuhns, C.S.J.
1914-2013

Acknowledgements

*With thanks to Chris Doran for his patience and generosity,
and to Lisa and Jeff Cragg, Yasmine, Jeffery, Kellan,
Peter B. Doran,
Jean-Marie Carlisle,
Joy Doran
Elaina Doran*

*Special thanks to Theresa Manriquez, M.Ed. for her work and support on the first edition,
to Jacqueline Anderson and Janet Martin for their friendship and wise advice and
to Carolyn Chard, Valerie Plancarte, and Kenneth J. Golick,
for their generous assistance with their time, effort, gracious enthusiasm, and encouragement.*

Self-esteem begins with the ability to read efficiently and fluently. Teach others how to read and their future will have no limits!
-Kent Looft
Design Arts

CONTENTS

Preface   *i*
    Important Background Information for Instructors
    Vowel and Consonant Charts   *ix*

Introduction: Instructor's Step-by-Step Directions for Teaching Phonics Steps to Reading Success   1
- Step 1: Teacher Reads.
- Step 2: Student Reads.
- Step 3: Spelling Quiz
- Spelling Instruction for Instructors
- A Note About the Importance of Handwriting

Chapter 1: Penmanship and Introduction to Decoding and Encoding the Code of the English Language   11
- Easy Steps for Good Handwriting
- Pre-Test and Post-Test Information
- We Must Understand a Little Bit About Codes
- How does the Language Code Work?
- When We Read, We Use the Code of the Language
- Short Vowel Sounds
- Basic Rule for Reading
- Basic Rule for Spelling
- Chapter 1 Review

Chapter 2: Introduction to Understanding Short Vowels and Reading Long Words   22
- Background Information for the Instructor
- Short Vowels
- Introduction of Troublemakers
- Poster: Read Left to Right
- The Clock Says "Tick, tock." (Words with –ck)
- Sound Spelling Sense
- Speed-Reading Game with -ack, -eck, -ick, -ock, -uck
- When is a Girl a Gril?
- A Little Background Information on Reading Errors
- Words with –le at the End
- Can You Read Long Nonsense Words?
- Chapter 2 Review

Chapter 3: Long Vowels and Vowel Teams   37
   The Team-Talker Vowel Story
   PSRS Color Code Explained
   Follow the "Shadow Game Rules"
   Team Talkers with Silent Shadow Vowels
   A Bit of History: Those Shifty English Vowels
   Variations of Pronunciations
   Team Talkers: ay, oa, ai, ie, ee, ue, ui, ew, oe
   Consonant Blockers
   The "Short" and "Long" of It
   Drill Instills; Practice Makes Perfect
   Silly Long Words to Enjoy
   Tips on How to Study Words to Spell Them Correctly
   Chapter 3 Review

Chapter 4: Some Historical Bits of How English Developed,   63
   Why We Have So Many Exceptions, Plus
   Helpful Hints for Handling Spelling
   and Reading Exceptions
   - Tricky and Sly Words Ending in Y
   - Y By Itself Says I
   - O at the End of a Word
   - Words That Are Troublemakers / Accents
   - A Note About "Sight-Word" Memorization
   - EA Words Can Be Troublemakers
   - A Little Inventive Spelling Causes Big Problems
   - Spelling Tips
   - Aw/au/ia/iu
   - Short oo and Long oo
   - R-Controlled Vowels: ar, or, er, ir, ur
   - Chapter 4 Review

Chapter 5: Decoding with Digraphs   89
   - The H Combos: ch, sh, th, ph, wh

Chapter 6: Confusing Concepts That Follow Rules   101
   – Most of the Time!
   - -ild, -ign, - igh, -ind
   - Time for Review
   - EUREKA! The *eu* and *ew* sound like u.
   - Silly Names: Read the Sounds; Follow the Rules
   - The Problem with Spelling OW! OU!
   - Meet the Silent –gh Team and –gh as /f/
   - Tall and Small

Chapter 7: Practical Strategies to Conquer Common Reading Challengers like C, G, Suffixes and Syllabication   116
- C -What Sound Does This Letter Make?
- Double C
- G -What Sound Does This Letter Make?
- C – H-Combo Trouble-Making Pretenders
- "Sh" Pretender Teams with -tion, -sion and -cial, -sial, -tial, -tious, -cious, -tient, -cient
- Syllabication Rules
- Diphthongs: oi/oy
- Take a Bite Out of Hard Words: Vowel Review
- When is the Final –ed Not a Syllable? – ted/-ded
- QU: The Romans Borrowed the Letter Q From the Greeks
- Y the Vowel?
- I Before E Except After C

Chapter 8: Prefixes Review and Preview   150

APPENDIX   176
- A. Post Script: After Students Have Been Through Phonics Steps To Reading Success, Then What?   177
- B. Reading and Comprehension Strategies   180
- C. Basic Rules of Phonics   185
- D. Glossary of Selected Terms   189
- E. Bibliography   190
- F. Index   191

PREFACE: Important Background Information for Instructors of Phonics Steps to Reading Success (PSRS)

Before you begin, you may have questions.
Whether you are an experienced teacher or you have never taught before, PSRS can help you to be successful in your teaching of essential phonics skills.

> ## "It doesn't matter where you come from; it matters where YOU decide to go!"

MOST OF US HAVE HEARD SOMEONE SAY, **"My child can read, but he (or she) has trouble with comprehension."** We may know adults who can read. However, they do not like to read or they have trouble with comprehension. You may be one of those adults. For *millions* of smart folks, reading (or spelling) is challenging.

The goal of reading is the accurate comprehension of an author's words. Why do so many read below the level at which should be reading with understanding?

To understand why a student might struggle with comprehension, it is helpful to imagine a student sitting on a three-legged stool. If all of the legs are of equal length and strength, the student will sit comfortably with ease. However, if one of the legs is weak or not as long as or as strong as the others, the student will labor to keep his balance, embarrassed at his wobbling. Should we consider the student to be *sitting disabled* or a *struggling sitter?* Clearly, the answer is no. Often, however, too many students are labeled as being "reading disabled" or as "struggling readers" when, in point of fact, the students are trying their best to use effectively the ineffective strategies that they have been taught.

When it comes to reading, the three essential *legs* of comprehension are:
- (a) **Accurate reading** of the written words;
- (b) **Understanding of the meanings of the words**; and
- (c) **Sufficient background knowledge**, including **grammar** principles *and* practices.

Pat Doran's PHONICS STEPS TO READING SUCCESS is *not* a complete reading program. However, it *is* a fast-paced, word-attack skills program. It quickly helps to build two essential skills that are necessary for successful comprehension: **accurate reading** and increased **vocabulary knowledge. PSRS does not teach phonics rules *as* rules.** PSRS provides **direct instruction** of phonics concepts **explicitly, systematically** and in a **fun** and **phonics-focused** format. PSRS also focuses on **spelling accuracy**.

WHY DO SO MANY PEOPLE HAVE TROUBLE WITH READING?

Over the past few generations, millions of students unsuspectingly learned to read using *unproven* and *experimental* reading methods. You may have been one of those students. Even today, instructional approaches are being used that reflect various reading-instruction theories that do not stand up to rigorous, scientific, research-based standards. These techniques may teach students to guess at words, use illustrations to "figure out" what a word might be, skip words, or memorize words by identifying the shape of each word as a whole unit.

Sometimes research-proven, effective strategies are looped together with less-than-good or even failed strategies. This is when educational theorists, working with publishing companies, combine ideas from various effective approaches with non-effective approaches to come up with "new" approaches, new products.

Nonetheless, there is a universe of data from long-term, rigorous, scientific research showing what is *most effective*. This approach requires the *direct, explicit* and *systematic* teaching of phonics concepts. A critical skill for students to develop is *phonemic awareness,* namely, the ability to learn about, think about, discern and work with individual sounds in words. Students also learn to blend sounds associated with the letters accurately from left to right, from beginning to end of the words. This is reading with phonics.

In the effort to get students reading early, however, instructors may teach a variety of combinations of phonics, non-phonics, *and* guessing strategies. Instructors may believe they are teaching phonics. This combined approach may *appear* to be effective early on. However, such an assortment of instructional strategies can lead to persistent errors and confusion. When students later employ these *error-causing strategies* to tackle reading tasks in upper grades, students frequently become *frustrated* or *resign themselves to failure*. Still others are *mislabeled* as being in some way *disabled*.

It may be that some of these students are skilled at using ineffective strategies learned in the primary grades. On the other hand, it may be that the students have developed their own "survival" strategies in trying to figure out how to read on their own. In classrooms, instructors expect students to read texts or to complete assignments with accuracy.

However, when students lack effective decoding skills, the confusion, errors, and frustration often enter as the student begins to guess. Without effective or corrective instruction, individuals continue to use ineffective strategies throughout their lives.

WHAT IS PHONICS AND WHY IS IT NECESSARY?

Reading English is like unlocking a code. Letters are symbols that stand for sounds. When we teach phonics, we are teaching the students to look at a symbol and say the sound that "goes with" the symbol. Therefore, the symbol b as in *bat* says /b/. There are 26 letters in the alphabet and approximately 44 sounds made from those letters or combinations of the vowels and consonants of the alphabet. These represent the basic phonics code of the English language.

A vowel is a sound of speech created by air passing in a continuous stream, **through an open mouth, with little or no obstruction** as **a, e, i, o, u**. A consonant is a sound of speech created by **stopping** and **releasing** the air stream as with the letter like p, **t, k, b**. *PHONICS STEPS TO READING SUCCESS* [PSRS] focuses *primarily* on the study of vowels.

When students read using phonics, they unlock the symbol-and-sound code of the consonants and vowels. This is **de**coding. When students use the code to write the letter or letters that "make that sound," they are spelling. This is **en**coding.

Of course, the English language is not "pure" English. It is a rich, fluid language, boasting the influence of many others, such as Latin, Greek, German, French, Old English and Middle English. Thus, many words in modern English cause trouble and do not follow standard rules. While the pronunciations of consonant sounds have remained relatively stable, the variations, pronunciations, and spellings of vowels within some words have *shifted* or changed over time.

Therefore, the culprits causing *most* of our problems in reading and spelling of English words are the variations in the pronunciations of vowels. PSRS is a word-attack program designed for students who know the consonant sounds. If students have difficulties, permit them to refer to the sound/symbol pages at the end of the Preface.

HOW DO STUDENTS LEARN THE WRONG STRATEGIES?

Anti-Phonics: As noted, non-systematic or non-explicit phonics methods suggest that students should memorize many words by their configuration or shape, that is, by *how they look*. Many classrooms have lists of *sight-words* posted. Such lists contain *high-frequency* words that regularly appear in books and reading passages. Examples of these words that appear frequently are *on, no, was, saw, in, it, if,* and *is*. This is *anti-phonics* since it is the opposite of decoding.

The practice of *sight-word memorization* was originally an offshoot of methods used to teach deaf students under the direction of the Reverend Dr. Thomas Gallaudet. Since students with hearing disabilities could not hear the letters' sounds that make up words, Gallaudet provided a workaround solution that focused on rote memorization of whole-words by their shapes or configurations as visuals representing pictures or concepts.

Sight-Word Memorization of Highly Irregular Words: Unlike the lists of hundreds of *sight-words*, it seems that the *highly* irregular words are relatively few in number. Most of the words that are considered to be highly irregular are indeed words that have only one or two parts that break the phonics rules or simply have a slight pronunciation variation.

Whole Language Philosophy: This constructivism approach teaches reading in a way that emphasizes learning whole words and phrases by encountering them in meaningful contexts, encouraging a meaning prominence rather than an accurate, decoding prominence. Some phonics may be taught. This viewpoint postulates that students use critical thinking strategies and rely on their prior knowledge to construct their own meaning of what the author wrote. Readers may guess at words, substitute words, or simply may skip unfamiliar words. Younger students may use invented spelling.

Hybrid Approach or "Semi-Phonics": Sometimes, students learn by way of a *hybrid* approach. In this way, they learn *some* phonics concepts, but learn also to rely on instant recognition of other words as whole units or as parts of words.

These strategies are examples of what the author refers to as **CAPs**: <u>**c**ommonly **a**ccepted **p**ractices</u> *without any validating, scientific research to support their use*. Unfortunately, many students carry the burden of having learned to read using a variety of experimental, ineffective CAPs that serve to *cap* the reading and academic progress of otherwise capable learners. CAPs create various types of *learned disabilities*.

Developers and implementers of these strategies do not *intend* for students to make mistakes. However, in the push to have students read too early and too quickly, students are encouraged to "read" books or passages long before they have acquired the phonics skills that are essential to read with accuracy all of the words in a given text. In response, students tend to invent their own "survival" strategies. Reading therefore becomes a slow, burdensome balancing act filled with frustration and weighed down with guessing and errors.

Often, caring and dedicated educators voice their concerns that they are working diligently and using reading programs packed with activities that are supposed to raise reading scores, but the scores remain stagnant or show little growth. Commonly, these programs and activities are based on theories but not on valid scientific research data. Just as CAPs cap student success, CAPs simultaneously restrict teacher success, as well.

INSTRUCTIONALLY DISABLED?

Often, when students learn to read using unproven and ineffective strategies, even otherwise capable students' tests or achievement scores may be low. This is especially relevant for students labeled as having reading or learning disabilities or for those who are *struggling readers* and are falling far below the acceptable reading level for their grade. Interventions that focus on reinforcing ineffective strategies, such as guessing, "echo-reading" or "parrot-reading," only serve to cement the error-causing inefficiencies. Regularly, intervention approaches serve only to modify grade-level materials or to make lowered accommodations for the reader's current abilities. CAPs fail to provide significant and effective instruction to correct what is erroneous or ineffective and to fill in what is lacking, in order to raise the reader's skill level. This can set up a series of circumstances whereby students with no actual learning disabilities become *instructionally* disabled.

CONFUSION ENTERS AND IMPEDES COMPREHENSION.

The consequences of deficient and ineffective reading skills learned in school become lifelong problems when these "error-causing strategies" remain identified and uncorrected. Therefore, it is necessary to provide readers with fast, effective, efficient decoding strategies at the very beginning of their reading instruction. On the other hand, if the damage is done, then explicit, systematic and direct instruction of effective phonics strategies must be the focus of intervention.

Conversely, when students learn the phonics concepts systematically through explicit, direct instruction, most struggling students can acquire the skills to blend letter sounds left to right and with an accuracy that will lead to fluency. Ultimately, with practice, the accurate and automatic decoding mastery will be in place. As a result, that "leg" of comprehension will be strong.

DOES THIS MEAN THAT LEARNING DISABILITIES ARE CORRECTIBLE?

If educational factors and not physiological factors are the reasons for the students' difficulties, the answer is yes. Note that in primary grades, the level of reading materials is strictly controlled. At first, the reading difficulties of a student may not be obvious. Words are still basic. Pictures and illustrations provide a number of visual clues. As noted above, this is one reason why non-phonics or anti-phonics strategies initially may *appear* to be effective.

However, as an individual advances through school and the reading material becomes increasingly more complex, comprehension *will* suffer. A student's test scores will fall far below his or her capabilities. In many cases, these students will assume that the problem is their own. Meanwhile, dedicated parents or teachers may assume that a student is *dyslexic, learning disabled,* or is prone to making mistakes or not trying hard enough. Indeed, **the reader *effectively* may be using the error-causing strategies that he or she has learned.**

One solution to this problem is to provide students with the tools to unlock the language code using phonics. Pat Doran's **PHONICS STEPS TO READING SUCCESS** program is a first step to better reading and comprehension that begins with the accurate reading of the written word.

When teaching older students, instructors must stress the importance of *unlearning* ineffective strategies and of *learning* to read phonetically. Still, **a few foundational steps are necessary regardless of a student's age or ability.** The teaching of the core skill set taught systematically will be the basis for continued success and will replace old, faulty strategies. Yet, old methods like guessing or substitution may be hard to unlearn. Patience on the part of teacher *and* student is essential.

DO I NEED TO HAVE A PHONICS BACKGROUND TO TEACH PSRS?

A teaching background is not necessary because PSRS is straightforward, foundational phonics information. Down through centuries from one generation to the next, skilled and unskilled individuals alike have been able to teach others to read with accuracy by using the foundational phonics code of the English language. With this in mind, PSRS is a teaching program designed for ease of use. Of course, the instructor must have a basic reading skill, but instructors who have taught PSRS often comment that they, too, learned much as they taught the program. On the lessons' pages, instructors with various skill levels will find useful tips they can use throughout the program. Whatever your level of teaching experience, whether it be widespread, narrow or nil, you will be successful in teaching your student(s) to read using PSRS. The instructional or teaching portion that you will read or explain to your student(s) is marked clearly, as is the portion of each lesson that students are to read.

In addition, it is possible for the instructor to create cards using a picture of a **b**at for the letter b pronounced as /b/, **h**at for the letter h pronounced as /h/, **r**abbit, and so forth. **Important note: If the student does not know the consonant sounds, the student must learn consonant sounds *before* beginning the program.** This book includes a chart with consonants and vowels following this page. PSRS Study Cards in a flip chart format are available for purchase (ISBN: 978-0-9771101-6-2). Learn more about the teaching of the phonics code of the English language and other information in *The Secret Club: Why and How We Must Teach Phonics and Essential Literacy Skills to Readers of All Ages* by Pat Doran, M.Ed.

Pat Doran's **PHONICS STEPS TO READING SUCCESS**

Vowel, Consonant and Other Sound/Symbols

Linguists tell us that "short vowel" **sounds** take less time to pronounce than do "long vowel" **names**. Thus, we have the terms, "long" and "short" vowels. Explain that the "short" and "long" diacritical marks over the vowels are used as pronunciation aids in the dictionary. Vowels are formed with an open mouth; consonants are pronounced by stopping and releasing air in various ways.
Refer to it as needed. Permission is granted to duplicate this chart.

Key words for sounds: **a**pple, **e**ggs, **i**gloo, **o**x, **u**mbrella/**u**p, **sh**oe, **ch**ips, **th**umb, **th**is, **aw**l, **au**thor, b**oy**. Long vowels in center column: the letters' name. This page of the chart is for reference *as* you teach PSRS. IMPORTANT: Do not have students memorize the chart before they learn the sounds in the PSRS.

/k/ ca, co, cu, cr…*

/s/ ce, ci, cy*

/j/ ge, gi, gy*

* Key words for sounds: **b**oy, **c**at, **c**ity, **d**og, **f**ish, **g**oat, **g**ym, **h**at, **j**ack-in-the box **j**umping, **k**ey, **l**eaf, **m**oney, **n**ails, **p**ig, **qu**een, **r**abbit, **s**on, **v**alentine, **w**agon, **b**ox, **y**o-**y**o, **z**ipper.
Note: Teach first the "hard" sounds of c as in *cat* and g as in *goat*. The "soft" c sounds plus ck, and ch are explained later in PSRS. X most commonly is at ends of words, pronounced /-ks/.
The letter x at the beginning of a word may sound like /z/ as in *xylophone* or "x" as in *x-ray*.
See other Edu-Steps materials at www.edu-steps.com.

INTRODUCTION
For the Teacher

Step-by-Step Directions
For Teaching
Phonics Steps to Reading Success

TEACHING PSRS IS AS EASY AS

PSRS IS A COMPACT, FAST-PACED PROGRAM FILLED WITH INFORMATION AND SKILLS' INSTRUCTION ON EACH PAGE.

The systematic, direct-instruction approach includes symbols to guide you as you teach *Phonics Steps to Reading Success*.

Note: PSRS is effective with one-to-one instruction or with small or large groups. For large groups, project page image on board or screen. Students must keep their attention focused on the board or screen as you teach. If students have PSRS POCKET PHONICS, the paperback version, it is best that students open their books only when you direct them to do so.

Step 1. TEACHER READS. 📖
This symbol means that the teacher reads until there is a ☆.

Step 2. STUDENT READS. ☆
This symbol means that the student reads (decodes) words until there is a 📖.

TEACHER AND STUDENT READ. 📖 +☆
These symbols together mean that the teacher *may* read along with the student.

Step 3. SPELLING QUIZ. 📝
Always give a spelling quiz when directed to do so.

T is a suggestion for an instructional strategy or other background information for the teacher.

Give a pre-test before you begin.

Assessments evaluate the degree of success – or lack thereof – of both teacher *and* student. You must give a test before you begin, so that you and your student will have a baseline, or a beginning score. A test given after completion of PSRS will tell you how much your student has improved. Additionally, a post-test will tell you how well *you* did as an instructor. Effective instructors analyze their own work and continually seek ways to improve.

PSRS is not aligned to any test. If you do not have access to assessments, consider doing an Internet research to find one of these free assessment options: (1) The National Right to Read Foundation, *Exploring: Resource Analysis Tools,* www.nrrf.org; (2) The *San Diego Oral Reading Assessment*; (3) *The Miller Word-Identification Assessment*, Edward Miller, 1991 & Donald L. Potter 2012.

Step 1. Teacher Instruction

☑ **When you see 📖, read instructional material clearly aloud.**
- Read with expression and enthusiasm.
  - If you are excited and positive about learning, your students will reflect your enthusiasm.
  - Conversely, if you are indifferent or lack energy in your instruction, your students may reflect that as well.
- Read the PSRS format.
  - When you see an underlined letter or letters, read them as their alphabet *names*, for example, a, b, c.
  - When you see the letters between slashes as /b/, read them as their *sounds*, for example, b says /b/ as in the first sound of *boy*.

☑ **Ask the students if they understand and/or have any questions regarding information in the instruction or lesson portion.**
- Students may understand more clearly, once they attempt to read.
- As needed, review concepts by returning to previously taught lessons.
- You may want to use your own or PSRS flashcards for a quick review of concepts.

Step 2. Student Decoding and Reading

☑ When you see ☆, facilitate the *fast-paced* decoding of the words and lists.
- **De**coding (reading) is going from symbol to sound.
- **De**coding is pronouncing the *sounds* of the letters as they appear in the word from beginning to end. (PSRS uses a simple one-sound-at-a-time approach, reading each sound from left to right, from beginning to end.)
- You or student should use a pointer or finger as a guide under or over *each* sound as it is pronounced from left to right and from first to last.
    - Do not place the pointer at the *middle* of the word.
    - Always start at the first sound of the word, then glide, left to right, to the final sound.
- If a student mispronounces a word, have the student read it with accuracy before continuing.
    - Give the student the chance to correct independently.
    - If a student is struggling, remind him/her of the concept.

☑ For the *first few* words in a list, you, as an instructor, may read along *softly with* the students as support and guidance, but <u>do</u> <u>not</u> read the words first and then have students repeat after you.
- There is value in recitation and "echo reading," but it is not the same as independent reading/ decoding.
- The goal is for students to be confident, independent readers, not dependent on someone else.

☑ Students must decode *aloud* as they read the words the <u>first time</u>. Do not have students pronounce or try to "figure out" words silently or softly to themselves first, then aloud.

Step 3. Encoding/Spelling

☑ **When you see ✏️, you are directed to give a spelling quiz of 3, 5, or 8 words.** (You *may* give one word at a time rather than 3, 5, or 8 at once. You may correct and analyze after each word.)

☑ **Remind students that spelling (encoding) words is much more difficult than reading (decoding) them.**

- There may be a "spelling overlap" as similar sounds may have different spellings such as:

    <u>ay</u> in *pay*   <u>ae</u> in *maelstrom*
    <u>ai</u> in *rain*   <u>eigh</u> in *eight*
    <u>a-e</u> in *pane*

- When we *read* any of these, they say the name of <u>a</u>: long <u>a</u>.
- However, when we spell the name of <u>a</u>, we will have to know from which of the options to choose to spell correctly the name of <u>a</u> for that word.
    - Refer to this as the "code overlap".
    - Scholars like Noah Webster and Samuel Johnson created standardized dictionaries or "codified" spelling and pronunciations.
- Often, old spellings have new pronunciations.
- People who know phonics are better readers *and* spellers.
- Students do not have to memorize whole words.
- As students read words in this program and later in life, they will identify those words that have *troublemakers*.

Note: For spelling quizzes, you may use any paper/pencil format. You may also want to purchase Pat Doran's *Phonics Steps to Reading Success SPELLING AND VOCABULARY JOURNAL* (ISBN-0-9771101-9-3) that is aligned to PSRS.

Step 3 continued: Spelling Quiz Directions

☑ **Always give a <u>short</u> spelling after each page or column when you see 📄✏️.** DO NOT OMIT SPELLING QUIZZES.

- Your students may use the formal PSRS SPELLING AND VOCABULARY JOURNAL that is aligned with this program or any "paper/pencil" format.
    - If you use keyboarding or other technology systems, you should also require learners to write the words by hand.
    - Hand/eye coordination that is required for writing by hand provides essential reinforcement for the brain that technology does not do.
- En**coding** is writing the letter(s) English requires for each sound.
- Remind students that they need to be **active readers** and, as they are reading, they should take note of spelling *troublemakers*.
- Learning to encode with accuracy takes more time and effort than does learning to decode with accuracy.

☑ **Follow Directions for 📄✏️ Spelling Quiz**

PSRS spelling quizzes have a two-fold purpose:
    #1: **To reinforce the phonics concepts.**
    #2: **To teach students how to study to spell with accuracy**.

- Pre-select 3-8 spelling words.
    - Select words at random, possibly choosing every other word or every third word.
    - You may ask the students to select words that they think other individuals may find to be challenging.
    - Help students to **pre-analyze** and to **identify troublemakers** as an instructional strategy to teach students how to study words for accurate spelling.
- Give the quiz.
    - Enunciate clearly; exaggerate, if necessary.
    - Repeat the word, as needed.

- Use the word in a sentence.
- During the quiz, have students say sounds with a soft voice, *sounding out* as they write letters from the beginning to the end of the words.
- It is *essential* that students pronounce the word aloud--slowly and quietly--to themselves as they encode, writing the letters left to right.
- By sounding out the word *as* they write the letters for the sounds, the students avoid the possibility of using whole-word guessing strategies in which the students remember what letters are in the word, but they do not know in what order they are to be written.

• Correct and analyze errors. Affirm success and/or progress.
  - Observe the students as they write, however, if you observe that the students are not doing well with several of the first three or four words, stop, review the concept, pre-analyze the words and continue.
  - If you give 3-8 words and the students encode with accuracy, go on to the next lesson.
  - If the students are struggling with the concept, you must stop, select a few other words from the list to pre-study. Then, give those words as you follow the procedure for the spelling quiz.

☑ **Allow students to self-correct by comparing their words to the correct words from the list.**

• Permit students to make their own corrections, either by crossing out the word neatly and writing it correctly next to the word (~~sep~~ *step*) or by correcting the error, perhaps by inserting the correct letter *(s^{t}ep)*.
• You may want to have students review aloud what they will have to remember so that they will be able to avoid making the error in the future.
  - Review the concept.
  - Take notice of *troublemakers*.

☑ **Ask which students achieved 100% accuracy.**

• One wrong? Two wrong? Who is improving?
• Congratulate success and progress.
• Students are "competing" with themselves to improve.

☑ **Ask for volunteers to share the words they got wrong.**
- Thank student(s) for volunteering.
- Explain that this helps *everyone* to analyze errors to become skilled readers and spellers.
- If students are uncomfortable about sharing at first, you may ask students to "make up" an error they think someone might make.
- Write the incorrect spelling where student(s) can see.
  - Example: The correct word is *tape,* but the student wrote *tap.*
  - You or a student can pronounce the word as written; ask: "What do we have to do to make a say its name?"
  - "What do I have to do to change *tap* to *tape*?"
- Analyze a few mistakes, thank students for volunteering and continue.

REVIEW

Accurate spelling requires knowing phonics concepts and exceptions.

Reading (decoding) is not as challenging as is spelling (encoding). Spelling requires more study and analysis. Some sounds have "code overlaps" which means that there may be several ways to encode (spell) the same sound.

-For **DECODING** (reading), when we SEE ai, ay, ae, a-e, eigh, we only have to remember to say the **name of a**.

- For **ENCODING** (spelling), when we HEAR the name of a, we must know which ai, ay, ae, a-e, eigh is required to be correct.

When we have students **pre-analyze** words, we must help them to know that there are parts that follow the code and parts that do not. It is important to help learners to analyze words and not memorize wholes.

Unlike the traditional *end-of-the-week* spelling quizzes with which most of us are familiar, the primary purpose of the PSRS spelling quiz at the end of each lesson is to reinforce the concepts that have been taught.

KEEP THE LESSONS MOVING QUICKLY!

Phonics Steps to Reading Success is the "**emergency room of literacy**". You must stop the "bleeding" before you begin the therapy.

In other words, **stop the students' use of inaccurate and inefficient word-attack strategies before you begin to focus on other skills such as comprehension**.

Many students may have major challenges because of their home situations, their personal problems, or the academic requirements in other classes. Without efficient reading skills, those challenges multiply. Most instructors have only a small window of time or opportunity to help students. Therefore, instructors, including those with little or no background in teaching phonics or reading instruction, must teach the basic phonics concepts quickly, efficiently, and effectively.

PSRS is designed to help instructors of all skill levels and academic disciplines to accomplish that important task in an average of 15 hours of instructional time. Obviously, young children, English language learners and some students may require more time. Still, PSRS is highly effective.

Just as the medical professionals in an emergency room save lives, you may save the educational, economic, and emotional lives of many individuals by giving them the "life-saving" literacy skills required for full and meaningful lives.

> PRACTICAL TEACHING TIP: As you teach PSRS, you may begin and end each lesson as your schedule permits, whether it is for five or fifty minutes. If you have to stop mid-page, simply make a note as to where you left off. Begin there next time. Simply, review the concept on that page before resuming the lesson.

A Note about the Importance of Writing by Hand

[T] HANDWRITING OR PENMANSHIP HINTS

The brain's "reading circuit" of linked regions that are activated during reading also is activated during handwriting, but not during typing. It has been also demonstrated that "writing letters in meaningful context, as opposed to just writing them as drawing objects, produced much more robust activation of many areas in both hemispheres." [1]

"Shadmehr and Holcomb of Johns Hopkins University published a study in Science magazine showing that their subjects' **brains actually changed in reaction to physical instruction such as cursive handwriting lessons**.[2] The researchers provided PET (Positron Emission Tomography) scans as evidence of these changes in brain structure.

"In addition, they also demonstrated that **these changes resulted in an almost immediate improvement in fluency, which led to later development of neural pathways.** As a result of practicing these handwriting motor skills, the researchers found that acquired knowledge becomes more stable." Dr. David Sortino, Brain Research and Cursive Writing.[2] [Emphasis added.]

---

[1] "What Learning Cursive Does for Your Brain. Cursive Writing Makes Kids Smarter." Published on March 14, 2013 by William R. Klemm, D.V.M, Ph.D. in Memory Medic
[2] Science 8 August 1997: Vol. 277 no. 5327 pp. 821-825
[3] http://davidsortino.blogs.pressdemocrat.com/10221/brain-research-and-cursive-writing/
Suggested: "How Should We Teach Our Children to Write? Cursive First, Print Later!" by Samuel L. Blumenfeld

Chapter 1

Penmanship and Introduction to Decoding and Encoding The Code of the English Language

📖 Throughout PSRS, you will be writing words. Handwriting is essential for brain development for reading and spelling mastery in a way that typing and technology are not. The brain's reading circuit is stronger when you write by hand. T If students use technology for spelling, reinforce with handwriting.

EASY STEPS FOR GOOD HANDWRITING

1. Hold a pen or pencil correctly.
2. Use correct muscle groups.
3. Hold the pencil (or pen) near the tip, *lightly* gripping it between thumb and index finger on either side.
4. Rest the pencil (or pen) on the middle finger.
5. Tuck the two remaining fingers under.
6. The paper is to be placed on the desk.
    a. The **right-handed** writer angles the paper so that the lower left-hand corner points to the center of his or her body.
    b. The **left-handed** writer angles the paper so that the lower right-hand corner points to the center of his or her body.

At the end of this section, practice following the directions by writing your name or other words.

7. Write all letters sitting **on** the line.
8. Write all tall letters the same height.
9. Write all small letters the same height.
10. Write all letters at the same angle.
    a. Straight up and down: IIII.   read
    b. Same slant for all letters: ////   read
    c. Do not mix slants: /I/I.   read

📖 Before we begin the lessons in PSRS, I will give you a pre-test to give us a baseline, which we will compare with a post-test that you will take when you have completed the PSRS program. We will see how much you have improved.

Yes, you will improve! *

📖 PSRS BUILDS SKILLS RAPIDLY.

This program may seem very basic to you at first. Everyone begins at the same starting point. PSRS is like an exercise workout program. When a trainer begins working with a client, it is important for the trainer to make certain that the client knows even the most basic steps correctly. Sometimes, the client may have picked up bad exercise habits or may have learned bad strategies that could limit advancement or even lead to injury

Similarly, this *phonics workout program* provides strengthening of your brain to develop your reading skills. It will help you to correct any bad strategies that may be limiting your success and teach you effective strategies. Look at the pages near the end of the program. In a matter of hours - not month or years - you will be able to read these words with confidence.

*T Give the pre-test at this point.

📖 WE MUST UNDERSTAND A LITTLE BIT ABOUT CODES.

📖 A code is an organized system of signs or symbols. Codes are the rules and an agreement about how you combine signs or symbols.

For example, Samuel Morse invented Morse Code that is a well-known code can be used instead of words in some circumstances. It uses on-off sounds, lights, or clicks that a listener or observer who knows the rules of his code can decipher or understand.

For instance, in Morse Code, the symbol for <u>s</u> is • • • and the symbol for <u>o</u> is - - -.

The most common distress signal is **<u>SOS</u>** or three dots, three dashes and three dots. If someone were using a light, they would signal by pressing the button on the light source three short times, three long times, and three short times.

The • • • - - - • • • is a code. It is recognized internationally by treaty or agreement. Anywhere in the world, people who know about Morse Code know that if someone is sending the <u>SOS</u> *signal*, it means they are in danger.

You may want to learn more about Morse Code on your own.

📖 How Does the Language Code Work?

📖 For us to understand the language code, let us use the following made-up code. Each symbol stands for a sound.

The symbol 🔲 represents the first sound in 🐯 (**t**iger)

The symbol ☑ represents the first sound in 🐂 (**o**x)

The symbol 👍 represents the first sound in 🐷 (**p**ig)

When we change symbols to make words, we decode. You can decode the following symbols. Write the letter for the symbol. Then, say the sounds to read the each word.

☆ 🔲 ☑ 👍   ___ ___ ___*

☆ 👍 ☑ 🔲   ___ ___ ___**

📖   Most people do not realize that, when they read and spell the English words, they are using a code.

The letters in the alphabet are symbols.

Each letter has a "sound" assigned to it.

Example: t is a symbol. When you see it, say /t/, as in *tiger*.

---
*top

**pot

📖 WHEN WE READ, WE USE THE CODE OF THE LANGUAGE.

The next few pages will introduce you to reading with accuracy by "sounding out" words using phonics and the PSRS program.

- As you read across, left → to → right, you must clearly pronounce EACH letter's sound.
- You will be reading the code.
- This is called "**de**coding".
- Your mouth changes shape as you decode each letter (symbol). Say the sound that is associated with the letter.
- Pronounce each sound, one right after the other.

📖 Decode these letter symbols.   /m/ /a/
Say the sounds associated with each letter.
Hold on to one letter's sound as you go to the next.
Do not take a breath or stop between each letter's sound. Blend the sounds. Let them *flow*, one to the next. As you decode the letters and blend their sounds, you read the words.

📖+☆   /m/ /a/ /z/ /t/

📖+☆   /s/ /p/ /o/ /t/

📖 Phonics is a code that is used by people in every country in the world. English is a popular language that is used worldwide for business, diplomacy, and general conversation.

"Short" Vowel Sounds

[T] *A vowel is called "short" because it takes a "short time" to say its sound.* Duplicate this chart as needed. The curve above the vowel is a mark used in dictionaries to indicate that the vowel is pronounced using its "short" sound. These marks are called "diacritical" marks. The letter (symbol) is represented by the first sound in the cue words. The teacher should read each line. Exaggerate enunciation. Have students notice how your mouth is formed. Students repeat. Long vowels (vowel names) are taught later in the systematic PSRS program. Do not have students spell words here.

📖 Throughout the program, we may look back to previous lessons for review, if necessary. For example, we can refer to the page of short vowel sounds.

📖 PSRS uses nonsense or not real, made-up words so that you learn how to apply what you are learning to any unfamiliar words you may encounter. Nonsense words provide practice using the concepts that have been taught.

For example, in the future, if you come across a long, unfamiliar scientific word, you will be able to "attack" it with the skills you learned in PSRS. In fact, the real and nonsense words in PSRS will prepare you to be able to read any of the almost 1,000,000 words in the English language. You will learn to use the English Language Code to read successfully.

In addition, there are exceptions or words that "break the rules," but PSRS will teach you to handle those when you encounter them, as well.

📖 Let us begin with the first foundational step of PHONICS STEPS TO READING SUCCESS. As you say each sound, hold on to one sound before you say the next as you change the shape of your mouth. You will be blending the sounds.

. Use a pointer or your finger <u>under</u> (or over) <u>each sound</u> as you say the sound for each letter, left to right, from beginning to end.
. Do not put your pointer under the middle of the word.
. Use your pointer to guide your eye as you decode.

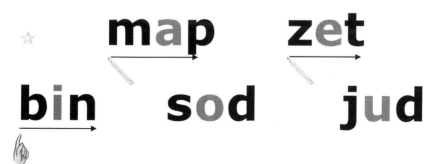

📖 THE BASIC RULE FOR READING (DECODING):

As you read, left → to → right,
clearly pronounce EACH letter's sound.

📖 Reading big words is the same as reading small words: one sound at a time.

- When you read, you are **de**coding, that is, going from letter to sound.
- When you read big words, notice how the shape of your mouth must change as each letter's sound is pronounced, one right after the other, across the word, left → to → right. Blend the sounds smoothly, one right after the other.
- If you need clues to remind you of the sounds, look back at the "Short Vowel" Sounds' cue page.

mapontazet

binrumsod

junitudimsan

📖 THE BASIC RULE FOR SPELLING (ENCODING):

As you write, left → to → right, clearly pronounce EACH sound as you write.

📖 Spelling big words is the same as spelling small words, that is, one sound at a time.

- When you spell, you are **en**coding: going from **sound** to letter.
- Spelling quizzes (📝) in PSRS give practice of phonics concepts and help you to learn to spell accurately.
- Say the sound(s) as you write each sound's letter symbol, left to right, from first to last, from beginning to end.
- Say the word slowly as you write the letters that represent the sound as in the nonsense word, *zet*.
  - Say the sound of /z/ as in *zipper*. Write z.
  - Say the next sound of /ĕ/ as in *egg*. Write e.
  - Say the final sound of /t/ as in *top*. Write t.

☆ **zet**　**map**

tik　pud　fon

Chapter 1 Review

- As you learn phonics, you will be able to read *decodable* text.
  - *Decodable* means that the text contains phonics concepts that you have been taught.
  - Sometimes, bright students may know the answers to questions they <u>hear</u>, but for tests or homework, they make errors.
  - Generally, if a student's phonics skills are not sufficient to <u>read</u> the questions with 100% *accuracy* and if the student misreads just one letter, he or she may change the entire meaning of the question.
  - For example, note how slight differences can change the meanings of words like *bond* and *blond*, *attitude* and *altitude*, or names like *Markeil* and *Makreil*.

- For PSRS Chapter Reviews, we will follow this procedure:
  1. I will read. I will say the word "blank" to substitute the answer.
  2. You will say the answer.
  3. Then, I will <u>reread</u> complete, correct statement.
  4. You may say the statement along with me, if you choose.

---

1. An organized system of signs or symbols is a _____.

2. As you say each sound, hold on to one sound before you say the next as you change the shape of your _____.

3. As you read across, _____ → to → _____, you must clearly pronounce EACH letter's sound.

4. When you read, you are <u>de</u>coding, that is, going from letter/symbol to _____.

1. code   2. mouth   3. left, right   4. sound

Chapter 2

Introduction to Short Vowels and Reading Big Words

T A Little Background Information for the Instructor

AS YOU TEACH, BE ON THE LOOKOUT! OLD HABITS DIE HARD!

GUESSING

Your students may have had exposure to "phonics" instruction. Be aware that many reading programs do not teach phonics systematically or explicitly. On the other hand, some use *leveled* reading materials, but not *decodable* reading materials.

Also, your students may have been taught to pronounce the beginning sounds in words and to look first within or at the end of words to find familiar little words or word parts like "word-families," such as *–at, -end, -ed*. Students may have been told to "figure out" what a word is based on context or illustrations. Often, students are told to *guess* at difficult words rather than to sound them out. This piecemeal approach causes errors, creates confusion, and impedes fluency.

Consequently, as you teach PSRS, you may notice that your students attempt to guess at words, to read only the first few letter sounds correctly, and to misread the rest. Readers may substitute whole words with words that may be "close," but not correct. For example, the students may read *brawn* as *brown* or *use* as *us*. No complicated analysis of the errors is needed here. Clearly, the students are not decoding accurately.

More than likely, the students are using strategies that they have been taught to use or have developed on their own. These ineffective strategies must be **unlearned** while, at the same time, the correct decoding strategies are **learned**.

INSTRUCTIONAL SUGGESTION: The beginning lessons may *appear* to be at a primary level. However, they are foundational and not to be skipped. PSRS systematically scaffolds concepts, building one upon the next. You may want to turn to pages 34 and 35. Explain that after a few short lessons, students will be able to read and spell these words with accuracy. In addition, you may want to refer to testimonies on back cover.

📖 A vowel by itself says its *short* sound. See Short Vowel Chart.	📖 Think about the SHAPE of your mouth as you say vowels.	📖 Read all sounds across. *Blend* sounds from first to last.	📖 Ox says, "Aah," NOT "Oh nO!" for these *short- O* words.	📖 After you read, this list, we will skip around for practice.
☆ **a**	☆ **e**	☆ **i**	☆ **o**	☆ **u**
fast	bent	fit	hot	dust
map	desk	if	pond	spun
flat	spent	it	Don	bump
trap	felt	in	fond	strum
Sam	lent	mist	lots	plum
tan	blend	slip	stomp	trust
cap	slept	twist	blond	trunk
clap	west	hint	font	grunt
clasp	pen	sip	prom	stun
damp	sent	strip	spot	hunt
ask	vet	split	pots	hut
lamp	vent	trip	stop	

📄✏️📖 I will pronounce the words. Ask me to repeat, if necessary. **Say the sounds aloud as you write.**

Mixed-up Short Vowel, Left-to-Right Practice

- Decode (read) each sound in the word in the order that it appears.
- Decode each letter's sound aloud to say each sound, from first to last.
- <u>Do not</u> read silently first. Just read aloud. Reread aloud as needed.
- Use a pointer to glide under each letter as you say each sound *aloud*.
- Let one sound "flow" into the next to *blend* sounds smoothly into words.
- **Do not add sounds! Do not leave out sounds! Do not guess!**

Names begin with CAPITAL letters. Identify names as you read.

☆

an	pond	swim	Pam
ten	pun	flat	bond
in	fin	Stan	trust
on		stump	ax
up		sip	
dent	Ted	snap	bank
fan	fond	fast	step
ask	blast	list	Ann
	flex	rust	flop
slat	bend		lap
bump	stand		it
fret	slot	rob	if
	plum	trap	fib
pin	blimp	stamp	Sam
stomp	pump	past	

📖 When you spell, say the sounds as you write. ✏️
Correct and analyze errors.

📖 The ™ usually stands for "Trademark". In PSRS, the ™ is a sign of a "trouble maker". A troublemaker can cause problems. When a **troublemaker** is introduced, it will be green or ™.

> *The*™*"* **is a TROUBLEMAKER! It says, "***Thuh***".**
>
> **Hint:** Generally, if "the" comes before words that begin with vowels, we say the name of e as in /thē/. Pronounce the as /thee/: the apple, the egg, the ox.
>
> To read these next passages, **blend** sounds into words. To blend, hold on to one sound as you say the next. Blend words into sentences.

T COMPREHENSION TECHNIQUE: You may have students illustrate this silly story.

☆ 1. **Ted sat on the bed. The fat dog sat on Ted. The red cat sat on the dog. The flat hat sat on the dog. The mat sat on the flat hat. Ted had a flat bed.**

📖 Do not guess at an answer. Find your answer in the passage.

☆ **Is the hat fat or flat?**   [ ] fat   [ ] flat
  Is the dog fat?   [ ] yes 👍   [ ] no 👎
  Is the mat on the hat?   [ ] yes 👍   [ ] no 👎

Answers: flat   yes   yes

☆ 2. **Stan is a big man. Stan has a problem. Bob is a fat cat. Bob is in the tub. Ann is a tan dog. Ann is not in the tub. Ann is on the bed. Bip is a mad cat. Bip is on a mat on the bed. Ann is on the bed. Bip is on the bed. Bob is in the tub. Stan cannot get in the tub. Stan cannot get on the bed. Stan just must stand.**

📖 Do not guess at an answer. Find your answer in the passage.

☆ **Is the cat in the tub?**   [ ] yes 👍   [ ] no 👎
  Is Bob the man?   [ ] yes 👍   [ ] no 👎
  Is Stan on the bed?   [ ] yes 👍   [ ] no 👎

Answers: yes   no   no

📖 Was this work difficult to do? To read long words, **blend** sounds across a word, left to right. Look for the troublemakers.

☆ **A n n i s o n t h e b e d**

This PSRS poster may be duplicated. Refer to its directives often.

1. **When you read words, read** (decode) **across** left→to→right.
2. **Read each sound** left→to→right.
3. **Do not skip any letters.**
   Use a pointer under each letter to help you read every letter.
4. **Do not guess.**
5. **Say each sound clearly and carefully.**
6. **Pay attention to the spelling of words as you read.** Look for troublemakers.
7. **Combine reading with spelling awareness.** Use a dictionary.

YOU WILL BE MORE CONFIDENT WHEN YOU READ AND WRITE.

📖 THE CLO<u>CK</u> SAYS, "T<u>ICK</u>, TO<u>CK</u>".

Spell with two letters: <u>ck</u>.
Say one sound /k/.
Can you read **short vowel**+**ck** sounds?
☆ /ack/ /eck/ /ick/ /ock/ /uck/

📖 Most words with a short vowel <u>and</u> /k/ sound at the end will have the –<u>ck</u> at the end. When you see an <u>s</u> at the end of a word as in *sticks*, the s changes the word from meaning a *single* (stick) to meaning *plural,* that is, more than one (sticks).

📖 When you read, pay attention as to how each sound is written. When you spell words with **SHORT VOWEL** + <u>ck</u>, write sounds that you hear *as* you hear them. As you take the spelling quiz for this page, underline <u>short</u> <u>vowel</u> + <u>ck</u> after you write each word.

☆ t<u>ack</u>	brick	stock	pluck
tr<u>ack</u>	speck	Rick	stuck
muck	rock	smock	sack
Mack	deck	block	ducks
flock	clock	Nick	pick
fleck	lock	mock	slacks
flack	pack	stick	
rack	tock	Mick	No spelling quiz .
neck	trucks	wick	

📖 SOUND SPELLING SENSE

1. **Take your time.**
2. **Think about the rules.**
3. **Say sounds as you write them.**

📖 Here is a word: **stick**. Read the sounds: ☆ s   t   i   k

📖 **SPELL CORRECTLY WITH CONFIDENCE AND ACCURACY.**

1. As you **say the SOUND   s** , write the letter <u>s</u>.
2. As you **say the SOUND   t** , write the letter <u>t</u>.
3. Then, think to yourself, "I **hear** short i sound and /k/. I must remember to write <u>ick</u>."

Remember: Short vowel + / k / are usually written as:

<u>a</u>ck   <u>e</u>ck   <u>i</u>ck   <u>o</u>ck   <u>u</u>ck.

📖 **PRACTICE SPELLING WITH NONSENSE WORDS.**

Use phonics to spell unfamiliar words. Use phonics concepts you have learned, such as short vowel + <u>ck</u>. **Avoid guessing and inventive spelling errors.** There is no need to memorize whole words. Pay attention as you read. Say each sound aloud softly as you write.

☆ 1. **pl o ck**   2. **bl i ck**   3. **sm u ck**   4. **sp o ck** 📝

T For the following spelling quiz, do not let students see words until spelling words have been written. Then, you should let students see each section to correct their own work.

📖 To pronounce and read WORDS clearly and carefully, you must pronounce each SOUND clearly and carefully.

T Spelling: 📝 5. **sick**   6. **stick**   7. **brick**   8. **smock**   9. **block**

📖 Speed-Reading Game
/ack/ /eck/ /ick/ /ock/ /uck/
Read accurately and quickly.

[T] This page may be duplicated for GROUP OR INDIVIDUAL practice or evaluation.

📖 We will focus on one set of words at a time. I will keep track of your errors and I will time how many seconds it takes for you to read each group of words above the gray scoring segment.
A word is counted as wrong *only* if you do not self-correct.
Strive for accuracy as being most important.
However, try to decrease your reading time each time you read.

☆ **sack sick sock suck**
back bick bock buck

| 16 possible | Reading time:____ | # right ____ | # wrong ____ |

rack Rick rock ruck
tack tick tock tuck

| 16 possible | Reading time:____ | # right ____ | # wrong ____ |

☆ **Mick Mack muck mock**
lock luck lick lack

| 16 possible | Reading time:____ | # right ____ | # wrong ____ |

pack peck pock puck
zuck zock zick Zack

| 16 possible | Reading time:____ | # right ____ | # wrong ____ |

☆ **zeck tick rock pack**
tuck back rock tock

| 16 possible | Reading time:____ | # right ____ | # wrong ____ |

dock Nick tock buck
lick track bick pock

| 16 possible | Reading time:____ | # right ____ | # wrong ____ |

☆ **stick stack tock stuck**
stock brack rock stuck

| 16 possible | Reading time:____ | # right ____ | # wrong ____ |

brick brack brock bruck
trick truck lick pock

| 16 possible | Reading time:____ | # right ____ | # wrong ____ |

☆ **Pick up the big black sticks. Stack the sticks on the rocks. Sit on the black sticks.**

| 16 possible | Reading time:____ | # right ____ | # wrong ____ |

📖 Can you increase accuracy and improve your speed a second or third time?
Achieve success by improving a little bit each time you do something!
Reading sentences is easier than reading lists of words, but reading lists of words is the drill that instills the concepts that will make reading sentences easier.

📖 Some students are taught to read and to spell by memorizing whole words by sight. This can cause confusion.

📖 Some worksheet activities for reading and spelling may have the students try to match words to fit into boxes. **Letters may be <u>in</u> a word, but in the <u>wrong place</u>!**
DO YOU THINK YOU ARE A BAD SPELLER? You may have learned to memorize words by their shapes. This can be confusing. See how the general configuration or shapes of the following two words are alike.

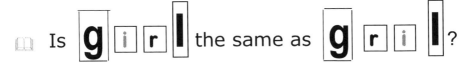

Do not be fooled by words that look alike or have the same letters. Do the words was™ and saw fit into the same boxes?

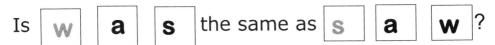

The letters are all lower case. There is a letter <u>a</u> in the middle. The letters <u>s</u> and <u>w</u> are on either end.

If readers do not read or write from **left to right**, it is easy for them to remember that there are letters **<u>a</u>**, **<u>s</u>** and **<u>w</u>** in the word. However, readers might not be able to remember the order in which the letters are to be written.

This may explain why some people write words using the correct letters, but put letters in the wrong places. This is common with words like **girl** and **gril** or **saw** and **was**™.

⊤ A Little Background Information for the Instructor: Reading Errors

Reading Strategies that Resemble Symptoms of Dyslexia

As students learn to decode, they may continue to try to read words as whole units. Similarities can be confusing. Strategies that aid students to focus their eyes on the letters, as they read left to right, can be in helpful in the effort to counteract dyslexia symptoms and other error-causing strategies.

A simple focusing strategy is helpful. Either you or the student should use a finger or pen or pencil point as a guide under (or over) the letters. Begin with the first letter in each word. Glide the pointer as each sound is pronounced, from beginning to end. As the student focuses on each letter, he or she can overcome a whole-word visual confusion and reversals.

CAUTION: Do not place the pointer over/under the *middle* of the word. This may have the student attempt to see the word as a whole.
If you are holding the pointer and the students misread the word, you may want to stop and not move the pointer. This lack of action indicates to the student that there is a mistake that must be corrected before continuing.

ERROR-CAUSING SIGHT-WORDS

The English language is a sound-symbol coded language and not a pictograph or logograph language. Therefore, reading instruction *must* be based on the code. The words to be recognized *by sight* should be limited to those that are *highly irregular* and do not follow the code.

The look-say method was developed to teach the deaf to read and does not use the English Phonics Code Lists like the Dolch List were developed when the look-say method failed with hearing students. The invalidated theory was that if the student is provided with enough opportunities to look at and repeat a word, he or she will eventually be able to read it automatically.

EXCEPTIONS TO THE RULES

Of course, some words do not follow the application of the basics of the phonics code. Other words are pronounced with regional or local differences that have evolved over many years.

PSRS provides strategies that may help to identify parts of words that do not follow code rules, otherwise identified in PSRS as *troublemakers*.

The English language vocabulary has upward of 1,000,000 words, nearly all of which are entirely or mostly decodable. When students are subjected to time-consuming drill on hundreds of high-frequency *sight-words*, students are hindered unnecessarily in their reading abilities and academic growth.

📖 Read a bundle of words with le at the end.
**You can read and spell correctly.
ALWAYS start at the beginning.**

If le is at the end of a word, just say /l/.
as in **bundle**. The e is ~~silent~~.

E at the end of any word with another vowel is
ALWAYS silent.

Words with **short vowel** sounds usually have two
consonants before the le, as in **bundle** or **meddle**.

❓ **WHAT?** Sometimes people think that **le** sounds like /ō/.
Say can-dle, **not** cand-o. Speak clearly to spell better.

T **Preview/pre-analyze** words that will be in the spelling quiz. For example, help to identify parts that would challenge like double letters and silent e. Give spelling quiz. Students check their own work. Analyze errors. Congratulate success.

☆bundle	crackle	sprinkle
handle	meddle	single
saddle	rattle	twinkle
settle	peddle	spindle
bumble	paddle	fiddle

We can add **-able** or **-ible** to verbs like **depend** or **flex**.
Words like *depend* or *flex* are a "part of speech" called
verbs. Some verbs are words that show action.

Do not double consonants when you add -able or -ible to **verbs**.

The **-able** and **-ible** are separate added endings. They are **suffixes**. Suffixes change verbs like ***depend*** and ***flex*** into describing adjectives: d**epend**able and **flex***ible*.

📖 A few hundred words ending with /l/ are spelled with –**el** like ***barrel, nickel, bushel, towel, pretzel***. Pay attention to –**le** and –**el** spellings as you read.

📖 CAN YOU READ **LONG NONSENSE WORDS?** Yes!

Some students are told to guess at a word.
GUESSING CAN LEAD TO MISTAKES!
FOLLOWING PHONICS RULES LEADS TO SUCCESS!

This exercise can help you to read each sound even in words that are long or unfamiliar to you. It provides practice by using CONTEXT to find word meanings.

CONTEXT means the parts of a sentence or paragraph that occur before and after a word or words.

Sometimes context will not be of help. It is a good idea to have a dictionary nearby as a handy reference.

1. As you read aloud, form your mouth to say each letter's sound in the order that it appears in the word.
2. Use a pointer under each letter to read left to right.
3. Let's review <u>le</u> at the end of a word. (End <u>e</u> is silent.)

☆ **s p a n f a n b i s u t t <u>l e</u>**

📖 Use context clues below to learn the meaning of this silly, long word.

> ☆Tom has a red pick-up spanfanbisuttle. It lacks handles and locks. It lacks gas in the gas tank. His spanfanbisuttle will not gō. It is his big problem. Tom frets.

📖 **What is it?** (Truck? A gas-powered vehicle?) What clues did you use? What do you think "fret" means? (Worry?) Is it a real word? Could you use a dictionary or just context to determine its meaning?

Read across from left → to →right.

sipswondundle

📖 Can you find the meaning for this made-up word by using context clues?

☆ The little black sipswondundle had six kittens.

📖 No one would have thought it was an apple, a table, or a pencil.

inexpressible

📖 Context helps. If the context clues are not clear for real words, you may have to use a dictionary. In the next passage, you will see troublemakers.
When you see to, say /**too**/.
When you see a as a separate word, say either its name /ā/ or /ŭh/.
When you see won, say /**wŭn**/.

☆ Sam Sladdle has won a grand trip to visit a ferry on the Mississippi. Sam will help on the ferry. He will go on the trip in Fall. Sam cannot express his vast happiness. It is inexpressible.

📖 1. Was he happy or sad? (Happy) A lot or a little? (A lot)
2. What clues did you use to decide? (won a trip, happiness, glad) How would the reader feel if that happened to him/her?)

35

Chapter 2 Review

📖 **For PSRS Chapter Review activities**, unless otherwise noted, I will read the statements and you will say the answer.

1. As you read across a word, from beginning to end, you must say each letter's _____.

2. When you read, do not add _____.
   Do not leave out _____
   Do not _____ at a word.

3. Nearly all words with a short vowel and a /k/ sound at the end will have the /k/ sound spelled as _____.

4. Context helps. For meanings of real words, if context clues are not clear, use a _____.

5. The following of the phonics rules leads to reading success. Guessing can cause _____.

6. If <u>le</u> is at the end of a word, just say /l/, as in bund<u>le</u>. The <u>e</u> is _____.

1. sounds 2. sounds, sounds, guess. 3. -ck 4. dictionary 5. mistakes 6. silent

Chapter 3

Long Vowels and Vowel Teams

Vowels are called "long" when we say their name as we read.

[T] Stories often are used to teach concepts. The following is an allegory or tale to help students understand about "long" vowels. Depending on your class and situation, the teacher should read **or** explain the story. The story is **not decodable**. This means it includes phonics concepts that the students have not yet been taught. Therefore, do not have the students try to read the story. Teachers of younger students may want to have students act out the story.

Additionally, PSRS introduces some **DIACRITICAL MARKS.** In dictionaries, you will see **diacritical marks** to help with the reader's correct pronunciation. In PSRS, the diacritical marks indicate a vowel's "short" sound as with /ă/ or "long sound" as with /ā/. If you are using a color version, a short vowel may be blue and a long vowel may be dark red.

Note: If you are using the black-and-white paperback version of PSRS POCKET PHONICS, the PSRS color-coding appears as shades of gray.

THE TEAM-TALKER VOWEL STORY

In an imaginary language land of letters, sounds, and phonics, we can create the instructional tale about team talkers.

The Background

In the land, vowels played by saying their sounds: /ă/, /ĕ/, /ĭ/, /ŏ/ and /ŭ/. At first, vowels were bashful. They would play alone and only said their sounds quickly. They did not play together. They were shy.

The Game Changer

One day, A accidentally bumped into letter E. The shy letter A apologized. E could see that A was very timid. E said, "Don't worry. Accidents happen."

A was happy that E understood and that he wasn't bothered. They began to talk. E was a colorful character who was confident and had a happy spirit.

E made up a game with A. At first, A was its usual shy self in the game. A only wanted to say its sound /a /, as in *apple*.

The vowel E was bolder and it had even more courage when it was with A.

E said, "I'll give you my courage." Then, you can say your name. I'll stand by you. Share my courage!"

E said, "Look for me when I follow you. I'll be like a silent shadow. When you see me next to you, I won't say anything, but you will have courage to say your name."

E added, "I'll be proud of you. You will talk for both of us. I will be silent. *You* will be the talker for our team. You will be the *team talker* and I'll be your silent **partner**."

They tried it, and it worked! With E's courage, A could now say its name, A.

Team Talker SILENT Partner

E acts like a shadow.
You can see it, but E is silent.

THE FIRST VOWEL OF THE TEAM DOES THE TALKING.

Thus, A and E became a vowel team.
A became the talker for the team.
E was the silent, shadow vowel.

Other letters in the land saw this game and they would say an old saying:

When two vowels go walking, the FIRST one does the talking.

Timid vowels joined in this *Shadow Game*. At first, many of them were too shy. They just said their sounds: /ĕ/, /ĭ/, /ŏ/, /ŭ/.

MANY VOWEL TEAMS, BUT THE SAME RULE!

In time, other vowels teamed up. The first teammate of every vowel team had courage. It did the talking and said its name. It was the TEAM TALKER.

The second teammate was silent. The second teammate could be seen, but it could not be heard.

Vowels often changed teammates. In these new *vowel teams,* the first vowel still said its own name: ā, ē, ō, ū or i. The second teammate was the silent shadow vowel that could be seen, but it could not be heard.

Their game will help you to read confidently.

> [T] PSRS color version uses a color code. In PSRS POCKET VERSION, colors appear as shades of gray.

> 📖 **BLUE** indicates the vowel's **SHORT sound**.
> **Dark RED** indicates the vowel's **NAME**.
> GRAY or ~~crossed out~~ indicates SILENT or no sound.

TOP SECRET! **Follow the SHADOW GAME Rules.**
Stay focused. You will be the winner!
The first vowel of the team is the **TEAM TALKER**.
It says its letter name, ā, ē, ō, ū, or ī.
The shadow vowel says ~~nothing~~.
SAY THE NAME OF THE FIRST VOWEL ONLY.

> 📖 IMPORTANT!! A **"long vowel"** says its **name**. Put a line over it as a sign of its *long* sound. **Cross out the** ~~silent~~ **vowel.** You may practice this by writing the word on another paper.

In the future, use the concept from this illustration below, as it may help you. You simply may visualize the marks and arrows.

Read each letter that is not silent. Here, you see five letters, but you will read only four sounds.

📖 Team Talkers with ~~Silent~~ Shadow Vowels

Say the name of the first vowel only. The second letter's sound is ~~silent~~.

☆ **āe   ēe   īe   ōe   ūe**

āy   āi   ōa   ēa   ūi

📖 The Team Talker is <u>ē</u> in the <u>ēa</u> Team.

I may read along softly with you for the <u>first few words only</u>. You must practice reading **independently.** You do not need to read the word to yourself first. Just read aloud.

☆
1. s ēa m
2. l ēa n
3. l ēa f
4. s ēa l
5. h ēa p
6. f lēa

bēam
tēam
drēam
bēak

bleak
steam
eats

📖 **EA Team Practice**

Use the trick of marking long and short vowels the vowels.

☆ **sēat**
crēam
Jean
speak
feast
treat

📖 Here is a bit of information to add to your background knowledge.

Capitalize direction words to refer to the **name** of part of the country as in **the East.**

New York is in the East.

Do not capitalize north, west, south, and east when they are used as **directions** as in **east.**

At the light, we will turn east.

📖 A Bit of History: Those Shifty English Vowels! *

Some ea words break vowel team rules.
They are part of the Great Vowel Shift.

T Depending on your circumstances, read or explain the following information. If students are *very* young, you may skip this page. Be certain that you read it for your own background knowledge.

📖 Before the development of the printing press that was used in England around A.D. 1476, words in the handwritten texts generally had been spelled as each particular scribe or writer wanted to spell them, according to the scribe's own social or regional dialect. There were no actual rules to follow. What would the exchange of ideas be like if there were no rules for us to spell or to pronounce words today?

After 1476, in England, spelling rules were created, aligned to or associated with how words were pronounced. The **GREAT VOWEL SHIFT** resulted in pronunciation changes of the vowels of English as they were spoken.

The Great Vowel Shift was widespread among many people who shared the English language. Some rules kept old spellings or pronunciations. This shifting of vowel pronunciation lasted from the 1500's through the 1800's and continues today to a lesser degree.

📖 VOWELS CAUSE THE MOST PROBLEMS IN READING AND SPELLING.

As the vowel shift continued, some spellings lost connections to how words had been pronounced. The pronunciation of vowels "shifted" in the mouth. The pronunciation of e may have "shifted" from ē to ĕ. Try to say the name of e and the sound of e. Notice the slight change in your mouth that is needed to say /ē/ and /ĕ/.   📖 + ☆: /ē/ /ĕ/

📖 or [T]   Some a or o sounds changed a bit over time. In some words, where a or o are lightly pronounced in unstressed parts, they sound like /ŭ/. This is symbolized as a pronunciation help *only in dictionaries* by an upside-down rotated e. We call this a **schwa e**. The *schwa e* pronunciation is the a in a*bout* [əˈbaot], o in *bottom* [bot əm]. Pronunciations changed; spellings did not. Use a dictionary or simply use what you learn in PSRS.

📖 or [T]   Irregularities between sound and spelling are a confusing bother. In the 1700's during the American Revolution era, even Benjamin Franklin was bothered. He developed a new phonetic alphabet to make spelling match pronunciation. Nothing much came of his attempts. At that time, Noah Webster did not like the irregular spellings either. He created a dictionary.

📖 or [T] **Some of his changes stayed with us.   Some of his changes did not.**

gaol ⟶	jail	ache ⟶	ake
mould	mold	soup	soop
honour	honor	sponge	spunge
centre	center	tongue	tung
humour	humor	cloak	cloke
publick	public	women	wimmen

http://www.merriam-webster.com/info/spelling-reform.htm

Variations

Readers often turn to the dictionary wanting to learn one precise pronunciation of a word only to discover that the word may have several pronunciation variations.

Because of local and regional dialects, English speakers around the world often pronounce words slightly differently. Many folks wish there were no exceptions. Have no fear! With a strong foundation of knowledge, you will be able to adapt.

Consider yourself to be in good company with those brilliant thinkers like Benjamin Franklin and Noah Webster.

Now you may begin to understand why we have words in various areas of the English-speaking world that have vowel parts that "break the rules". For example, in Standard American English, we say:

brĕad, thrĕad, wĕather, hĕad.

However, in other places, some may say:

brēad, thrēad, wēather, hēad.

DON'T WORRY. When you are reading without someone help, you may have to try both pronunciations. As you go through PSRS, you will learn more about these rule-breaking **troublemakers**.

📖 The Team Talker is ā in the āy Team.

T Use color coding and diacritical marks. Do not use echo reading.

📖 Read the words in this column slowly at first. Repeat more quickly, if needed.

☆
1. stāy
2. pāy
3. trāy
4. grāy
5. Māy

📖 **PRACTICE WITH THE ĀY TEAM.**

Read across from left to right.

Read each sound.

Do not skip any letters.

Let the letters be in charge.

No guessing!

☆ brāy
stray
grāy
away

splay
way
prēpay
clay
Clayton
play
———
essay
fray
nay
display
dismay
mislay
sway

lay
slay
day 📄✏*

📖 <u>Ay</u> says /ā/. However, you may hear <u>aye</u> sometimes said as /ī/ as in the following:

"The gruff pirate said, 'Aye-aye, Captain.'"

***T** Spelling hint: For review, perhaps add one or two words from earlier lessons. As always, pre-analyze, study, preview, practice and review as necessary. Capitals are for names only.

📖 The Team Talker is ō in the ōa Team.

T Use color coding and diacritical marks. Do not use echo reading.

📖 Read the words in this column slowly at first. Repeat more quickly, if needed.

1. flōa̶ t
2. rōa̶ st
3. gōa̶ t
4. sōa̶ p
5. fōa̶ m
6. bōa̶ t

📖 PRACTICE WITH THE ŌA TEAM

Show the silence of a shadow vowel. Draw a line through the 2nd vowel.

Draw a line over the vowel that says its name.

This is a **"diacritical mark"**. Diacritical marks are in dictionaries to help us pronounce words.

Green dots below indicate the sounds that you sound out. There are four letters, but only three sounds. Read across the word.

☆ g ō a̶ t
 •   • •

s ō a̶ p
 •   • •

📖 Point under each sound as you read each sound left to right. Replace bad habits with good ones.

☆ ōats
fōam
rōast
moans
groan
toad
coat
toast
floats
load
goad

T SPELLING QUIZ REVIEW

1. **Teacher and students review encoding: going from sound to symbol.** Spelling takes more focus and study than does decoding, going from symbol to sound.

2. **Teacher and students review the concept.** Students explain new concept. Example: "O in oa team says its name. A is silent."

Preview and pre-analyze a few words for quiz.

Pay attention to vowel teams and to troublemakers.

3. **Teacher says words clearly and slowly.** Exaggerate as needed.

4. **Student says the word ALOUD while writing each letter of the word from first to last.**

5. **Analyze errors.** 📖✏

The Team Talker is ā in the āi̶ Team.

Read the words in this column slowly at first. Repeat more quickly, if needed.

1. f āi̶ nt
2. p āi̶ nt
3. strāi̶n
4. s āi̶ l
5. m āi̶ l
6. sprāi̶n

Practice with the āi̶ Team.

Say the first vowel's name. The second vowel is a ~~silent~~ **shadow** teammate.

☆ tail
bail
taint
raid
hail
rain
rail
drain
stain
vain

sail
wail
wait
snail
gait
waist
train
hail
paint
trail

braille
(Named after Louis Braille.)

contain
maintain
explain

These next sets of words show the change *one thin letter* can make.
The first word has a short vowel.
The second word has the ai vowel team.

☆
1. Brad
   bra i̶d
2. pal
   pa i̶l
3. pad
   pa i̶d
4. mad
   ma i̶d
5. rad
   ra i̶d

The Team Talker is ī in the ie Team.

1. p ie
2. t ie
3. f ie
4. v ie
5. cried*
6. tried*

*📖 **ABOUT VERBS:** A verb is a part of speech. It can be an action word. "**Present tense**" means that the action it is happing *now*. "**Past tense**" means the action already happened. *He cried. We tried.*

Verbs that end in y are in the *present* tense. You can change to the past tense.

"**When there is a word ending in y, change the y to i and add -ed.**"
Read ie as a vowel team.

| spy → spied |
| cry → cried |
| dry → dried |

📖 **PRACTICE with the ie TEAM.**

die	fried
tried	lie
tied	fie
spied	dried
vied	plied

implied

📖 **BONUS WORD:** Follow the color code to read this word:

belie

📖 It means to give a false impression. Example: *His nervous shaking belied his calm voice.*

Sometimes ie ™ at END of words says /ē/, as in Marie. We will learn more about exceptions later.

📖 Pactice with the <u>ee</u> Team

☆ m ēe t

f ēe t

sl ēe p

d ēe p

strēet	slēe t
feet	flee
reek	sleek
steel	eel

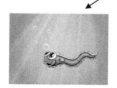

Greek →
seek
meek
seem
creek →
asleep*

* 📖 S<small>CHWA</small> ə <u>R<small>EVIEW</small></u>:

    In dictionaries, you will see a letter as an upside down <u>e</u>: ə.

    In American Standard English say /**uh**/. *Asleep* may be shown as /ə-sleep/.

    If you are reading aloud and are not sure, simply follow phonics rules you know. Just read /ă/*sleep*. You will be correct.

    What may happen is that you may have variations of British, Irish or other English-based accent. If you are reading aloud, you can be confident that you are accurate.

    Schwa ə in dictionaries indicates pronunciation, but is not in other print materials.

📖 The Team Talker is ū in ūe, ūi, and ew™ Teams.

In some places, people may use a **strong long u for** a **ui** team.

In the U.S., we often read *ue*, *ui*, *ew* with a little bit more /oooo/ sound.

Regional accents may be different.

Try reading the words both ways. You may notice a bit of an accent!

☆ **dūe**

stew

drew

frūit

Sūe

📖 Practice with the ūe Team

For these words, ue = /oo/.
☆
blue glue
true clue

📖 For these words, <u>ue</u> = /ū/.
☆ **cue**
rescue
value
continue 📝

📖 Sometimes two vowels are in words. They look like vowel teams. Pronounce each vowel quickly, but separately.

☆ **du·el** [du·el]
cru·el [kru·el]
fu·el
gru·el

📖 Practice with the ūi Team

<u>Ui</u> in the next word sounds like /oo/. *

☆
suit
fruits
suits
suitable
fruitless

📝

*There are other <u>ui</u> words with different pronunciations. Dictionaries help.

📖 Practice with the ew Team

or these next <u>ew</u> words, say /oo/. ☆

new /n/ /oo/
flew
crew
Andrew
Drew
Lewis 📝

📖 For the next words, say /ū/ or /y/u/ for <u>ew</u> or <u>ue</u> as in **hew** /h/yū/.

☆ **hew**
few
a**skew**
Tuesday

📖 Use the rules you know or use a dictionary. Either way you say /oo/ or /ū/, you will be more correct than if you skip, guess at or substitute the whole word.

📖 The Team Talker is ō in the ōe Team.

📖
Remember the rules and use diacritical marks.

☆

d ōe
t ōe
al ōe
s ōe

John
D ōe

P ōe

📖 Practice with the ōe Team

☆ **woeful**
Joe
foe
ōboe
toenail
roe
floe
goes
does™ /duz/

📖✏️

📖 **Warning:** Some vowels are together and *look* like vowel teams, but they are sounded separately.

☆ **dū-et**
pō-et

📖 or T A Bit of History

Some names may have been popular in the past. Some have changed, but they reflect their origins.

For example, Chi (/kī/) is the name of the 22nd letter of the Greek alphabet. It is written as X, x in the Greek language.

The ch in the name below is pronounced /k/. The name usually is pronounced with two syllables, **Chlō · ē**.

Chloe's origin is Greek and means "blooming".

📖 Practice with Vowel Teams

☆ **seam**
coat
pail
foam
clean
suit
stew
meet
tried
trait
tree
toe
fruit
feed
Tuesday

📖✏️

The Team Talker is ā in the āe Team.

The ae team is not used often, but you must know it. These appear to be hard words, but just read any word one sound at a time. Look for vowel teams. **Note: If c is at the end of a word, pronounce it as /k/.**

☆ **Āeson**

Dāemon

Hāeman

maelstrom

tāel

Gāelic

📖 Can you identify proper nouns or names?

📖 **Practice with all of the vowel teams.**

☆ **dream**
gray
goat
contain
sundae
Sunday
tied
replied
fleet
rescue
suit
Drew
essay
woeful

Gaelic
spied
tied
aloe
mail
foam
goal
maelstrom

📖 Do not memorize words by their shapes. Study spelling by analyzing the word.

How do we do that? For example, pay attention to ae in *sundae* and the capital S and ay in *Sunday*, ue in *rescue*.

CONSONANT BLOCKERS

📖 Sometimes a consonant is between a vowel and its silent shadow teammate e.

A consonant tries to "block" the *strength* of the silent shadow teammate e from getting to its vowel teammate.

The consonant tries to "split" the vowel team.

The strength of silent SHADOW teammate e can get past 1 blocker.

This means that e's *strength* still can get past **1 consonant**. When you read the words here, the **first vowel** of the vowel team says its name. The final e is silent. Blend consonant and vowel sounds from left to right, from first to last.

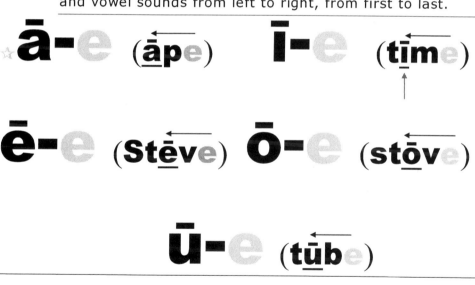

📖 The **ONLY TIME FINAL E IS SPOKEN** is when it is the **ONLY VOWEL** in the word, as in the word she. Then, **e** says its name as in:

☆ **he   me   be   we**.

📖 TEAM TALKER with Consonant Blocker Practice:

Sometimes a consonant will try to get between the silent shadow teammate e and its vowel teammate. The blocker consonant cannot block e's courage. **The first vowel will still say its name.**

 **Pay attention to this following information.
It is very important!**

A, E, I, O, U are vowels.
☆ **E is the ONLY one of these vowels that can send its courage past a consonant blocker to a teammate.** ☆
Oh, yes, the letter y is used both as a consonant and a vowel. We will learn more about y later.

cān~~e~~
mān~~e~~
pāne
plane
Pete
snipe
time

hide
hone
ride
rote
kite
pale
bite

plate
stripe
tape

SPELLING QUIZ REVIEW:
·Guide student through review of lesson's concepts.
·Pre-analyze words.
·Give 3-5 words.
·Correct and analyze errors.
·If student is successful, go to the next lesson.

📖 This is the SHORT and L O N G of it!

Careful practice makes perfect! Look for silent <u>e</u>. If it is helpful for you, you may pronounce just the vowels first. Then, read the words. Names begin with capital letters.

1. can cān~~e~~
2. bit bite
3. man mane
4. pan pane
5. plan plane
6. pet Pete
7. snip snipe
8. Tim time
9. hid hide
10. rid ride

11. rot rote
12. kit kite
13. pal pale
14. bit bite
15. not note
16. tot tote
17. slim slime
18. hop hope
19. strip stripe
20. tap tape

📖 **DRILL INSTILLS! CAREFUL PRACTICE MAKES PERFECT!**

fast	grump	beast	not
bed	bet	steam	note
pond	stripe	pain	same
mist	main	pad	kite
fret	flake	paid	pane
dust	flack	deep	rid
ape	lump	sleep	ride
track	Ben	suit	dream
blue	truck	flue	speak
teal	block	hew	relay
hope	stale	floe	float
Ed	candle	tael	week
pin	span		waist
pen	brick	ax	Jane
glue	pluck	tax	few
spent	twinkle	ask	street
trust	goal	Kate	boat

SOME SILLY LONG WORDS TO ENJOY!

The long words on this page are **decodable** which means that you have learned the phonics facts you need to read them.

Sometimes, illustrations that are on pages help us to figure out <u>meanings</u>. **Do not rely on illustrations** to figure out what a word <u>says</u>. For example, the illustration on this page is of *no* help.

DO NOT GUESS! Guessing at what a word says can lead to mistakes. Guessing gets in the way of correct understanding of what the author wrote. Be confident. Take your time.

Change the form of your mouth to say each sound (phoneme) in the order it appears in each word.

Do not say the last <u>e</u>'s name. Also, remember that <u>e</u> at the end cannot send its courage past <u>two</u> blockers.

☆ **pr<u>ai</u>tz a nm<u>ay</u>z e p p l e**

☆ Ted woke up and went to eat. He drank coffee and ate fried eggs and toast. He had sweet praitzanmayzepple on his toast.

Use the context to figure out the meanings. **With real words**, if context does not help, **use a dictionary**. What context clues tell you what he put on his toast?

T **Woke up, egg, coffee, sweet, toast.** It was breakfast. Praitzanmazepple could be butter, honey, jelly. Answers may vary.

☆ **veckl<u>ai</u>z i n z o p m<u>ae</u>p l e**

T If necessary, the instructor may read along **softly** with student for minimal support.

☆ Last year my granddad was 100. We had an event for his vecklaizinzopmaeple. People came. We had fun and ate cake. He had 100 red candles on his vecklaizinzopmaeple cake. We gave him gifts.

T Identify context clues: **fun, cake, gifts, candles.** (Was it his birthday?)

If you can read this 19-letter word, you can read ANYTHING!

No ✏ for this page.

📖 THIS PAGE HAS TIPS ON HOW TO STUDY WORDS FOR CORRECT SPELLING.

1. As you read left to right, hold on to one letter sound as you blend it with the next. In a similar way, as you spell, say the sounds slowly as you write the word, one letter at a time, from beginning to end.

☆ **praitzanmayzepple**.

📖 See vowel teams <u>ai</u> and <u>ay</u>. Both say /ā/.
Pay attention to **what** the vowel team is and **where** it is.

- See that the <u>ai</u> team is first and <u>ay</u> team is second.
- How many <u>p</u>'s are there near the end? (Answer: 2)
- How is the /l/ sound at the end spelled? (Answer: <u>le</u>). 📖✏

📖 As you spell, always say the sounds quietly as you write. Watch for troublemakers and vowel teams such as <u>ai</u> and <u>ae</u>. Remember <u>what</u> and <u>where</u> they are.

2. Now, read the next word and explain aloud how you would analyze this word to study it for correct spelling:

☆ **vecklaizinzopmaeple**

📖 What do you have to remember? Analyze aloud.
☆ I will… [Student explains.]

📖 Did you identify the –<u>eck</u>, <u>ai</u>, <u>ae</u>, <u>le</u>?

Always PAY CAREFUL ATTENTION as you analyze letters and teams that may cause you problems. 📖✏

Chapter 3 Review

📖   I will read the question. You provide the answer.

1. When two vowels go walking, the _____ _____ one does the talking.

2. Sound out these vowel teams:
   ☆ ae, ai, ay, ee, ea, ue, oe, ie

3. Do vowels or consonants cause us the most problems when we read or spell English words?

4. The <u>schwa ə</u> is used in what reference book to help explain the standard pronunciation of some vowels? It does not appear in other reading materials.

5. Out of the vowels, A, E, I, O, and U the ____ is the ONLY one of those vowels that can send its courage past a consonant blocker to a teammate.

1. first   2. a, a, a, e, e, u, o, i.   3. vowels   4. dictionary   5. E

Chapter 4

**Some Historical Bits about
How English Developed,
Why We Have So Many Exceptions,**

**Plus Helpful Hints for Handling
Spelling and Reading Exceptions**

📖 I SEE THE PLANE FLY IN THE SKY.

Tricky and sly words ending in y.

📖 **READING:** When you see a word with **y at the end** plus at least one other vowel in the word, the y says "eeee".

- The e at the end of a word with a consonant blocker will let the vowel teammate say its name as in **babe**.
- The y at the end acts like a ~~silent~~ *shadow* e at the end because it will let the vowel say its name as in **baby**.
- Two consonant blockers between the vowel and the final y keep the vowel from saying its name as in **sorry**.

📖 **SPELLING:** If you hear "*eee*" at the end **and** if there is another vowel in the word, write the "*eee*" sound with y: **dizzy**.

ONE CONSONANT BLOCKER: If you want to write a word that ends in the sound "eee" as in baby, say /b/ /ā/ /b/ as you write. Then, for the "eee" we hear at the end, write y: **baby.** *Baby* is never written b-a-b-e. The e at the end is ~~silent~~.

S O R E does NOT say SORRY. What does it say? ☆**sore**

📖 **TWO CONSONANT BLOCKERS** keep the vowel's *short* sound. If there is just *one* consonant, you must DOUBLE the consonant to keep the vowel sound *short*.

📖 + ☆ *Kīty* is not *kitty*. *Būny* is not *bunny*.

| ☆**happy** | **tricky** | **sadly** | **fifty** | **sassy** |
| **lādy** | **bāby** | **sunny** | **fuzzy** | **sixty** |

Y by itself says I!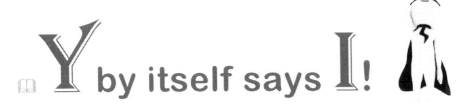

When Y is the **only vowel** in a word, say the name of I.

☆ **my dry cry fly sly**
sky by spry fry sty

Review: If a **Y** is at the end of a word that has **another vowel**, say the **name of e**. Two blockers make vowels say their short sounds.

☆1. The funny, fuzzy tricky bunny is sly as it sits by my tīny bāby.

2. The man was happy and spry as he drove his dandy new car.

3. A sly spy sat in the plane to fly and try to apply his sneaky skills to trap the crafty bad man.

4. The spry, sassy puppy rapidly ran to my flat boat to see it float by him.

QUICK MEMO: When you see the <u>o</u> at the end of a word, say its name as in these words:

☆ g**o** n**o** s**o** tomat**o**   potat**o**   sol**o**   hell**o**

Troublemaker reminder: **to**   ☆ I will go to the store.

> 📖 Some folks say English is hard to learn because so many words or parts of words break the rules. We can say that these words are "troublemakers".
>
> **PAY ATTENTION!** These next few pages may help you to understand why some words break the rules. The more you know, the more you can grow!

SOME ENGLISH SPEAKERS MAY SAY WORDS A BIT DIFFERENTLY THAN WE ARE USED TO HEARING.
WE MAY SAY THAT WE HEAR AN *ACCENT*.

> **Accent**: An accent is a way of speaking. Specific groups or residents of an area may pronounce words a bit differently from you.

- You and I might pronounce <u>come</u> as /kŭm/.
- *Some may say that this shows an* **"American accent."**
- People from other English-speaking areas may say /kōme/.
- People pronounce words with variations or differences.
- Some people who speak English may pronounce a few vowels, consonants or consonant clusters differently than we do.
- In addition, people from various areas may stress different syllables or parts of words differently.
- Although English speakers around the world may have "accents," we can understand what they are saying.

> 📖 **Some words are very old troublemakers!**
> **They *turn away from* or *break the rules* that we are learning.** These words have changed. That is because some of these words have been in use for over 1,000 years. **If you lasted over 1,000 years, you might change a little, too!**

📖 THE SAME LANGUAGE TREE: DIFFERENT ROOTS AND BRANCHES

The troublemakers you will encounter may be words that have common beginnings or *roots*. They have different branches or stems.

> 📖 **You are learning**
> **STANDARD AMERICAN ENGLISH.**

- Follow phonics rules that you are learning in this program. Sometimes, words "break the rules".

- When you follow the phonics rules you learn, what might happen is that your speech could have traces of some other English-language influence such as that of British, Scottish or Australian.

- However, English speakers will understand you.

🔊 or 📖 CHALLENGES OF LEARNING ENGLISH AS A SECOND LANGUAGE

For people whose first language is not Standard American English, some words or sounds may be difficult to pronounce. Let's find out why that is so.

- When babies are first born, their muscles are flexible.

- As babies begin to speak a language, they use only those particular muscles of the mouth that are required to pronounce the words and sounds of their language.

- Any muscles in the body that are not used become weak–even those in the mouth.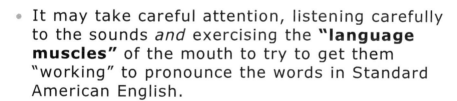

- It may take careful attention, listening carefully to the sounds *and* exercising the **"language muscles"** of the mouth to try to get them "working" to pronounce the words in Standard American English.

- You should strive for accurate pronunciation.

- Use a mirror as you practice, if necessary, to help you see how your mouth is shaped to pronounce the sounds.

- Practicing to say the proper sound will result in accurate pronunciation.

🇹 or 📖 A NOTE ABOUT "SIGHT-WORD" MEMORIZATION

The method of using *sight words* is based on a picture/sight-word system developed by Reverend Dr. Thomas Gallaudet to teach deaf students how to read by *sight*. They identified the words by their shape instead of using phonics rules to decode or "sound out" the words left to right, from beginning to end.

cat

The system was eventually adapted to teach hearing students to learn lists of "sight words". Instead of using pictures, teachers tell students what the word says. Students repeat the words and learn to identify the word by its shape, not sounds.

if
it
in
is

This so-called *sight-reading* causes problems. Words like *is, if, it, in, on, an, a, was* and *saw* can often be confused if the reader reads quickly and does not decode each sound left to right. Most of these high frequency words are decodable all or in part.

If a reader is *not* paying attention, he or she may read or say **in** instead of **on**. Simple mistakes can cause confusion in comprehension. See how one misread word can change the meaning of a sentence.

1. *The dog is **in** the house. The dog is **on** the house.*
2. *I am **in** today.   I am **it** today.*

Students who are trained to use phonics concepts effectively are able to read long, unfamiliar words correctly. However, even these students may misread the little words that have been memorized "by sight". This can cause problems.

A <u>very few highly irregular</u>, frequently used words may be learned by sight. Examples are **do**, **the**, *to, want, have.*

📖 **PRACTICE!** Let's read troublemakers **do, the, have** and **want** in sentences. Generally, it is better to practice "sight-words" in sentences than to memorized words in lists.

☆ **Do** you see **the** dog? I **have the** cat. I **have the** cat.

📖 A troublemaker often is taught as a "sight word" to be memorized. However, only **part** of the word actually "breaks" the rules.

E A WORDS CAN BE TROUBLEMAKERS!

Some ea words do not follow the vowel team rule when we speak. Say the short sound of **e** (ĕ); a Is silent.

EXAMPLE: The word *heave* follows vowel team rules. Although, when you see the word *heavy*, do not say "hēavy". Say "heavy".

You may need to rely on a dictionary for words with ea.

Let's try a little creative acting! Listen for an accent when we read these sentences below using both pronunciations.

☆ **ready** ☆ **"I am ready to go."**
📖 Other English dialect: "I am rēady to go."

☆ **instead** ☆ **"I want milk instead of candy."**
📖 Other English dialect: "I want milk instēad of candy."

☆ **heavy** ☆ **"The big rock is heavy."**
📖 Other English dialect: "The big rock is hēavy."

☆ **bread** ☆ **"Do you have milk and bread?"**
📖 Other English dialect: "Do you have milk and brēad?"

📖 **come** /kum/   **move** /moov/
☆ **"Please, will you come and move the desk?"**

📖 Various Internet websites teach how to speak with different dialects.

📖 PRACTICE WITH SOME TROUBLEMAKERS

In life, there are *people* who do not like to follow rules! They cause us troubles. On this page, practice reading *words* that cause trouble. These are words with <u>ea</u> that say /ĕ/.
With information and practice, you can overcome troublemakers!

CORRECT SPELLING IS NECESSARY!

You can be a good speller. You must <u>study</u> how the words are spelled! Combine reading/spelling awareness.

- WHEN YOU SPELL, write each sound as you hear it.
- WHEN YOU READ, pay attention to how words are spelled.
- Notice where TROUBLEMAKERS are in the words.

☆ready	instead	heavy	move
come	tread	bread	meant

📖 Troublemaker *to* says "too" *as in, "Go to the store."*
Troublemaker *of* says "uv" as in, "The man is on top of the rock."

☆ 1. The little pile of rocks is not _____.

2. He had to_____ from Texas to Maine.

3. We like to play golf _____ of tennis.

4. I will get milk and _____ at the store.

5. Can you be _____ to go Monday?

6. The _____ on my back left tire is bad.

7. I _____ to ask you if you want milk or tea.

8. Please _____ to my home?

Answers: 1. heavy 2. move 3. instead 4. bread 5. ready 6. tread 7. meant 8. come

T or 📖 A Bit of History: Old Spellings

READ OR EXPLAIN: Scholars are people who do research. Etymologists are scholars who study about the origins or the beginnings of many English words. Some dictionaries give word origins about which etymologists know. Look at some of these words below. This page shows some original spellings -- mostly Old English (OE) -- along with today's spellings. We can try to read them.

📖 or 📖 + ☆

1. **active**
   actif

2. **they**
   thei

3. **your**
   eower

4. **promise**
   promys

5. **buy**
   buyen

6. **parents**
   parens

7. **shove**
   scufan

8. **above**
   a + bufen

9. **weather**
   weder

10. **wear**
    werian

11. **what**
    hwaet

12. **the**
    se, seo,
    thaet,
    thy

13. **head**
    feafod

14. **would**
    (OE) wolde
    (Archaic)
    wouldst

15. **feather**
    fether

• As found in READER'S DIGEST OXFORD COMPLETE WORDFINDER, 1996 Oxford Univ. Press.

📖 A few exceptions come from MIDDLE ENGLISH. In these modern words, the a says its own name.
☆

pāste   wāste
haste   tāste
hāsty   tāsty

📖 **Wow!** You do not need to carry a stack dictionaries around with you to become a good speller! I have a better idea!

📖 BE CAREFUL!
A **little** inventive spelling (guessing) causes **BIG** problems.

- School prepares students for their future.
- Businesses often ask people to fill out job applications.
- Poor spellers do not get hired for many jobs.
- Work hard so that you will become a good speller.
- People will respect your ability.
- You will be more confident when you write.

📖 Example: 📖 +☆ **I like to eat bread and butter.**

📖 We can review words with <u>ea</u>.

eat: The <u>ea</u> in *eat* follows the vowel team rule.
bread: The <u>ea</u> in bread is a *troublemaker*.

- The <u>ea</u> breaks the rules.
- The first vowel DOES NOT say its name.
- It says its sound /e/ (*egg*.) The <u>a</u> is silent.

📖 **SPELLING TIPS**: There are ways to handle spelling troublemakers. Today, we can learn two.

#1

📖 Pronounce a word as it usually is pronounced in Standard American English. Example: bread

Say: **brĕad**

You must remember any **troublemakers** or ~~silent~~ letters, what and where they are.

📖 Think to yourself or softly say /brĕd/.

📖 Below, dots show you which sounds are heard. The **arrow** points to silent spelling **troublemaker a**.

☆ **b r ĕ a d**
• • • ↑ •

You **must** make a "mental note" to remember **what** and **where** a troublemaker is.

📖 Explain how we could use Strategy #1 to spell these words correctly.

📖 +☆ heavy instead come

#2

📖 Pronounce the word following *regular* phonics rules. Example: bread

Say: **/brēad/**

It may *sound* odd to you to say **brēad** *as you spell*, but this trick may help you to spell correctly.

📖 Think to yourself or softly say /brēd/.

📖 When you say **brēad**, you will hear the name of ē and you must remember that e needs a teammate for e to say its name.

So, in *bread,* remember to put in the silent team member, a **after e**.

Remember silent teammate or troublemakers. Example: move. Think /mōve/ so you would remember the ō and ~~silent e~~. Explain how we could use Strategy #2 to spell these words correctly.

📖 +☆ heavy instead come

☆ **Hi! I'm Tricks!**
   I'm here to help!

📖 **If spelling words are still giving you trouble, help is on the way!**

📖 Pay attention to **troublemakers** in words.
Pay attention to **who** and **where** they are.

TRICKS can help you spell a word correctly!

Look for surprising TROUBLEMAKER TRICKS.

Did you know that there is a **lie** in **believe**?

Did you know that there is an **ear** in your **heart**?

Follow the rules. Remember your *favorite* tricks.
For example, read *fa -vor-it,* but spell *fa-vor-īte*.

- I have a **friend** in the end.

    You might want to say and spell: *fri* - end.

- Another word for perspiration is **sweat**.

    It looks like **swē t**. It says **swĕ t**.
    As you spell it, say the SOUNDS that you
        HEAR and remember to put in a after e.

Review strategies from page 74 as needed.

Simple Spelling Strategies for Most Words
1. Write letters from left to right for each SOUND you hear.
2. You only have to remember the **troublemakers.**

📖 *Read from left to right* ⇒ ⇒ ⇒ ⇒ ⇒ ⇒

Read sounds from left to right.
Read words from left to right.

The activity below reminds you to read from left to right. Do not skip.

You are playing the letters' game.
Follow their rules. It's their game!

☆ **pail, paid, man, Sam, the, for**
pail the for man paid the Sam
Sam paid the man for the pail.

📖 Do not skip around or leave out words.
. It is the same for sentences in this activity.
. It is the same for *anything* that you read.
. Read left to right. No skipping!

☆ **sky, kite, can, I, the, see, the, in**
sky in the kite the see I can
I can see the kite in the sky.

📖 **His picnic was rained out. We say, "AW! That is sad!"**

When you say the sound of /aw/, shape your mouth like an oval egg.

Say, "Aw, aw, aw!"

ALWAYS → read → from → *left* → to → *right*.
- DON'T SKIP! DON'T GUESS.
- LET THE WORDS AND LETTERS BE IN CHARGE.
- IT IS THEIR GAME. READ BY THEIR RULES!

📖 THE AWESOME ™ TEAM

EXTREMELY IMPORTANT! To pronounce /aw/, form your mouth in an OVAL or egg shape as you say the /aw/ sound.

If you have a problem, you may want to pretend to have a hard-boiled egg in your mouth as you say aw words.

Read these aw™ words. Read across. Say each sound from first to last.

☆dawn	fawn	lawn
saw	awful	sprawl
tawny	bawl	brawn
draw	craw	straw
raw	flaw	pawn
law	gawky	drawn
awl	hawk	

📖 You may want to watch my mouth as I pronounce each word for spelling. 📖✏

📖 **Au is another aw sound!**
Au requires an oval mouth shape.

- **Ar**thur is a name.
- An **au**thor is a writer.
- **Ar**thur is an **au**thor of books.

Notice one word below with "silent" letter n. As you read, you may see an asterisk (*). Look for a **matching asterisk**. Usually, it is found near the bottom of the page. It gives information.

☆ **auto**   **haul**   **autumn**   **applaud**   **Paul**
   auk   **Aubrēy**   **Audrēy**   **Maud**
automobile*   Au'·gust **   au·gust' *

📖 USING A DICTIONARY CAN INCREASE YOUR VOCABULARY AND READING SKILLS.

📖 rec ol **lect´**: **to remember**
    ☆ I recollect many happy events.

📖 **rē´**- col lect: **to collect again**
    ☆ I will try to re-collect the money.

📖 **com´** press: **a soft pad to apply cold or hot**
    ☆ Put a cold compress on his sore ankle.

📖 **com press´**: **to press together, condense**
    ☆ Compress the jacket to fit in the backpack.

📖 * This word is commonly pronounced as *au-tō-mō-bele*.

** In the dictionary, accent marks show STRESS or force. Accent marks (') indicate which syllables we are to stress. A **syllable** is any one of the parts into which a word is divided naturally when it is pronounced. Sometimes dictionaries show the stressed syllable in **bold.**
*** Words that are spelled alike may be pronounced differently with a different syllable stressed.

TROUBLEMAKER ALERT! IA and IU

These troublemakers look like vowel teams, however, it is a tricky disguise!

When <u>a</u> is at the end of a word, it usually sounds like /ŭ/ as in *banana* and *panda*.

Sometimes <u>i</u> comes before <u>a</u> or <u>u</u> in a word, as in <u>ia</u> or <u>iu</u>. These are NOT the same as shadow vowel teams <u>ai</u> or <u>ui</u>.

With <u>ia</u> or <u>iu</u>, the <u>i</u> will sound like the long ē (tree) sound. The <u>a</u> or <u>u</u> will say the short u (up) sound.

ia sounds like ēŭ

- Lid<u>ia</u>
- Austr<u>ia</u>
- battalia
- Austra<u>lia</u>*
- mēd<u>ia</u>
- trivia
- via

iu sounds like ēŭ

- mēd<u>iu</u>m
- pōtass<u>iu</u>m
- pent<u>iu</u>m
- sōd<u>iu</u>m
- fōl<u>iu</u>m
- millenium
- rād<u>iu</u>m **

** Remember to help students to pre-analyze words.

---

* People in the United States might say **Aus·trā·lia**.
People in other places might say **Au·străl·ia**.
Local or regional pronunciations may be slightly different. Spelling:

📖 When you say au or aw, remember to make your mouth the oval shape.

Stop! Do not run away.
You can do this!

☆1. I s<u>aw</u> the dog's sore p<u>aw</u>. He had to cr<u>aw</u>l on the l<u>aw</u>n.

2. The l<u>aw</u>yer had a hobby. He tried to dr<u>aw</u> the sunrise at d<u>aw</u>n.

3. I did hear the sick baby b<u>aw</u>l.

4. The ball hit Jim in the j<u>aw</u>. It was <u>aw</u>ful.

5. Seals often can be seen in austere frosty sites on our globe.

6. Paul had to haul the author's boxes in his auto in the autumn.

7. Maud and Audrey saw him in Austria and Australia in August™.

📖 In the next sentence, you may pronounce the word *aunt* as "ant" or "<u>au</u>nt". Either is acceptable, based on local, regional, or family preference.

☆8. Aunt Jan had to applaud Pete. He is an author.   📄✏ At least one sentence dictation.

📖 "SHORT" oo: foot

☆ **took**
nook
stood
look
wood
good
soot
brookside*
cook 📖

📖 Words with this oo sound:
☆ **should, would, could.**

📖 These words are from Middle English and Anglo-Saxon spellings like *scheolde, wolde.* Example from Canterbury *Tales. Prologue. Line 310:* **And gladly wolde he lerne, and gladly teche.**
Sometimes, poets used a spelling like *couldst*.

📖 "LONG" oo: moon

☆ **soon**
boom
boot
goose
foolproof*
stool
baboon
bamboo
spooky
hoop 📖

📖 This page is an example of the influence of word origins, dialects and local accents.
There is a small difference in the /oo/ sounds. The sound depends on how and where the words developed.

📖 ***C**OMPOUND WORDS*: two words joined to make one word.
☆ **inside, raindrop, footprint, bedtime.** Optional 📖

CONTROL YOUR CAR! Look for r-controlled vowels.

 📖 Control your c<u>ar</u>! Some vowels **change their usual sound when followed by an r.**

- When you try to say ă as in apple + /r/ as /ă/ /r/, it may feel a bit uncomfortable to pronounce.
- Say /ah/ /r/ when you read. Write <u>ar</u> when you spell.

HELPING CLUE: Underlining the /ar/ sound can be helpful.
- The sound of the letter <u>r</u> is like the sound of a growling dog. Say, "Grrr" not /ruh/.
- When you see or hear the <u>r</u> in a word, think of a<u>r</u>m.

☆ **<u>ar</u>m**
b<u>ar</u>
f<u>ar</u>m
barb
Barb
y<u>ar</u>d
st<u>ar</u>t
dart
h<u>ar</u>m

☆ **sp<u>ar</u>k**
tarp
hard
lard
far
tar
cart
card
yarn
lark

📖 **<u>Ar</u>e you sm<u>ar</u>t about <u>ar</u>?**
It would be **SMART** to have a spelling practice test with these "*r-controlled*" vowels.

o + r = or   fork

This is easy! When you see the OR Team,
always, always, always say, "OR".

f**or**
t**or**n
b**or**n
f**or**t
h**or**n
p**or**t
st**or**m
l**or**d
morn
store
format
stork
sort
sport
n**or**mal
organ

forlorn
Horton
Morris
forget
conform
doctor
afford
harbor
absorb
endĕavor™

 Review and pre-analyze words for correct spelling.
Pay attention to troublemakers.
- Read *Hortŭn*, but you may exaggerate and say *Hortŏn* to spell (encode) correctly.
- Remember ĕa in *endeavor*.

A Bit of History: "English Blend"

T READ OR EXPLAIN THE FOLLOWING.

 The English we speak today may be compared to tea that is brewed using leaves from several tea plants. The many flavors of tea are the result of different combinations of several types of tea leaves.

Example: When we read **er, ir, ur,** we say /ur/.

Why do we not hear short vowel sounds in er, ir, and ur?

Many sounds have come down through history and began around an area we know as England with a language we call *Anglo-Saxon*.

English today is actually a blend of many languages.

- The earliest Anglo-Saxon language was a blend of dialects of some groups living along the British North Sea coast. That early English [Old English] was constantly changing. *

- Sounds for spellings of er, ir and ur may have been said by some people clearly pronouncing the short vowel sounds as /ĕr/, /ĭr/ and /ŭr/, but we pronounce all three sounds of er, ir and ur as the *general* sound we hear in *fur*: /ur/.

- Over the years, the sounds seemed to sound the same as we hear them in Standard American English today.

- Some people around the world still pronounce these sounds with short vowel sounds of /ĕ/, /ĭ/ and /ŭ/.

- Americans, Australians, people from the United Kingdom and other English-language speakers can understand each other despite the various dialects; we use an almost identical spelling system.

- As you read, pay attention to how words are spelled.

***T** Its usage covered 700 years in Britain in the 5th century to the late 11th century, sometime after the Norman invasion. You may want to do more research on your own.

er

says /ur/

<u>S</u>**e**rve the tea. **S**erve the ball.

☆ mann<u>er</u>
term
herd
fern
verb
serpent
servant
perform
alert

never
after
perk
ever
offer
aberrant
blunder
vertigo
jittery

☆ The jittery zookeeper made a blunder. He was not alert. He lost the aberrant serpent.

Optional:

ir says /ur/

Stir the tea.

☆g**ir**l	sk**ir**t	st**i**rrup	fl**ir**t
st**ir**	sw**ir**l	f**ir**	**ir**k
f**ir**m	g**ir**ls	sm**ir**k	tw**ir**l
s**ir**	d**ir**ty	b**ir**l	t**ir**l
b**ir**d	sk**ir**ts	aff**ir**m	
w**ir**l	v**ir**tue	inf**ir**m	

🆃 Students may need to use a dictionary.

☆1. The girl did not <u>irk</u> her mother when she continued to <u>tirl</u> the car handle, making a rattling sound.

2. The bird had a <u>firm</u> bite of the worm.

3. It is a <u>virtue</u> not to <u>smirk</u> at the mistakes of classmates.

Optional: 📝

ur says /ur/  I see rabbit f<u>ur</u>.

☆ **fur**	**turf**
bur (or **burr**)	**hurdle**
hurt	**absurd**
burn	**blur**
burp	**blurt**
turn	**cursor**
spur	**hurl**

☆1. The toddler began to overturn his purple grape juice drink into the purse of the nursery nurse. The nurse did not blurt out. She was not stern.

2. The bank clerks tried not to murmur, chuckle, or smirk at the robber and his silly, absurd fake fur mask.

Optional:

The -ēre, īre and -ūre follow **VOWEL TEAM** rules:

☆ h<u>ere</u>   f<u>ire</u>   adm<u>ire</u>   p<u>ure</u>

Chapter 4 Review

📖 I will read the question. You provide the answer.

1. When you say the au/aw sound, make your mouth shaped like an oval or the shape of an _____.

2. The next two sentences give suggestions for two different ways to help us do something better.

   a. "Say the word by following ALL of the rules that you know, however, remember silent letters."

   b. "Say the word as it is commonly pronounced in Standard American English.

   These suggestions may help us to _____ better.

3. Read the following words: ☆ term, flirt, burst

4. How are these following letter combinations pronounced in Standard American English? ☆ Ere, ire, ure.

5. What is a compound word?

6. English today is actually a blend of many _____ over centuries. As a result, we have many exceptions or words that *break the rules*.

1. egg   2. spell (or encode)   3. /ur/   4. ēre, īre, ēre
5. Two complete words joined as one   6. languages

Chapter 5

Decoding with Digraphs

 ☐ or 📖 ## A Bit of History: The Development of Our Alphabet Was a Group Effort!

The Early Alphabet: N. S. Gill writes, "Semitic people from the eastern coast of the Mediterranean (where Phoenician and Hebrew groups lived) are usually credited with developing the world's first alphabet. It was a short 22-character list with (1) names and (2) a fixed order for characters that could (3) easily be memorized." *What Was the First Alphabet?* N.S. Gill, About.com *

The Greek Alphabet: The Greeks added vowels.

A B Γ Δ E Z
H Θ I K Λ M
N Ξ O Π P Σ
T Y Φ X Ψ Ω

http://stehlsavidge1.wordpress.com/2011/03 © <a

The Roman Latin Alphabet was like ours, but it was lacking J, U and W. Romans traveled widely, conquering people and building many things. They chiseled words in stone and on walls. The C and the G often were not clearly different. **

They had used I for I *and* J, and V for U *and* V. Today we have three additional letters in our alphabet: J, U, *and* W. See how J and U are similar in part. Say the name of W. The W was written by using the letter v twice: vv. The name of **W** reflects that it was once a ***double u***.

*http://ancienthistory.about.com/od/language/f/1stalphabet.htm
**http://www.dreamstime.com/jasmina_info#res2263150

THE H Combos

📖 or 📚 A Bit of History:

"Necessity is the Mother of Invention"

In places where people did not have a written language, as we know languages are written today, people often used picture symbols to represent the sounds in their words.

For example, in some places, the sound /th/ that we now hear in "<u>Th</u>ank you" was shown or written as a picture of a thorn.

When the Romans conquered anyone, they ordered the people to write their language using the Roman alphabet. The Romans did not have a /th/ sound in their vocabulary.

So, for example, the two Roman letters <u>t</u> + <u>h</u> were used as symbols to represent ONE SOUND: /th/.

Because of **usage**, **place of origin**, sometimes **misunderstanding** or **poor writing**, we now have two letters written for a particular sound.

These are called **digraphs:** di (two) graph (write).*

*Pay attention to correct pronunciation.
  Di·graph is often **mispronounced** as di·a·graph.

📖 **We use two letters to write one sound. The letter h was used to make many digraphs, as with ch, sh, th, ph, wh.**

C+H as in CHOO-CHOO /CHIPS

Pronounce ch as the STRONG /ch/ sound as in *choo-choo* and *chips*, not soft *shoo-shoo*. If you have difficulty in pronouncing /ch/, it may help to practice ch by saying "Choo-choo chips."

Strongly stress the ch in *Choo-choo*. **Immediately**, say "Chips." Say, "Choo-choo chips, choo-choo chap". Practice is important for success.

☆ choo-choo
chap
chain
chop
charm
chart
chomp
chill

chin
chunk
cheese
cheek
Charles
Chester
checker
churn
cheap

cheep
branch
charter
chimpanzee
artichoke
chimney*

📖 * Do not say or spell *chim · i · nēy*. Read and spell **chim · ney**.

> 📖 **When a ch sound follows a short vowel, you MUST have a blocker!**

For example, in the word **ranch**, the **n** acts as a blocker. **If there is no blocker, put a t-blocker between the short vowel and the ch.** In the word *match*, the t is put in to act as a blocker. It slides into the ch sound as /tch/.

> **EXAMPLE: Do not write** *mach*.
> **No blocker? Put in a t-blocker. Write:** *match*.

Top Secret! When a ch sound follows a vowel team, you do not need to add blockers.

☆ **ditch**

peach
📖 Peach has a VOWEL TEAM No blocker needed.

ranch
trench
stretch
match
Dutch

roach
latch
catch
switch
glitch
poach
fetch
sketch

📖 IMPORTANT! Pay attention to how these words are pronounced and spelled. Often, they are confused.

☆ **A pitcher pitches the ball.**

See the pitcher of water.

A picture hangs on the wall.

LOOK FOR:

1. Long vowel teams
2. *-tch* words
3. Other blockers!

☆chin	latch	archery
stitch	merchant	satchel
poach	teacher	dispatch
catch	hutch	batch
reach	bleach	fetch →
hatch	bench	arch
trench	church	📖 watch
ditch	crunch	
stretch	coach	
sketch	pitch	

Often, when <u>a</u> follows <u>w</u>, we pronounce <u>a</u> as /ah/ or /ŏ/. ☆

waddle
wand   want
wad   water

T ✏️ Pre-analyze and give 3-5 words. Correct and analyze errors. Repeat steps as needed.

REVIEW RULES

Long vowel teams have **no blocker** before <u>ch</u>:
  ☆ **peach, bleach**

Short vowels have a **blocker**:
  ☆ **flinch, ha<u>t</u>ch**

If there is **no vowel team** and **no blocker**, put a <u>t</u> before you write <u>ch</u>:
  ☆ **ditch, etch**

TROUBLEMAKERS: ☆ **lunch͜eon**™

For words with **<u>wr</u>** at the beginning, the **w** is ~~silent~~.
  ☆ ~~w~~**retch**   ~~w~~**ristwatch**

SOME EXCEPTIONS: No blockers!
  ☆ **rich   such   sandwich**

OTHERS: -dge words Blocker rules apply: -dge says /j/.

☆ **ridge** /rij/ **sludge**   **bridge**   **grudge**

lodge   **fudge**   **ledge**   **edge**

📖 **This man will** *sh-sh–sh-shi*ver when he *sh-sh-sh-sh*ovels snow!

Why does *sh* NOT say the sounds /s/ /h/?

🎩 *A Bit of History:* Read or Explain

📖 In 1066, William the Conqueror defeated the English king, Harold II, at the Battle of Hastings, and changed the language as well as the government of England. Probably, about that time, the sc was pronounced as /sk/. The sk was changed to sh over time. Now we have the /sh/ digraph. _{STORY OF ENGLISH: Mario Pei, 1952, p. 84.}

Could changes have happened because of careless handwriting? We can't blame it on a computer spell-check program!

☆**sh**ip	shampoo	mesh
sheet	shudder	swish
sheep	Shelley	shush
shōre	shrub	shuck
shun	should	usher
shirt	sheen	vanish ✏️
shade	hush	📖 CHALLENGES!
shame	dash	☆seashore
shrimp	rash	marshmallow
		mushroom
		dashboard ✏️

T or 📖 A Bit of History: Digraph **th**

It started thousands of years ago. Before the Romans ruled, the *th* sound was written by using the picture of a thorn. When the Roman armies took over lands and peoples, the Roman *a/b/c/d* alphabet replaced picture symbols.

The /th/ sound found in non-Roman languages had to be written with two letters because the Romans did not have /*th*/ in their language. Over time, two letters, t + h came to represent the spoken sound of /th/.

Now we have the digraph t + h or th /th/ that has two slightly different pronunciations: the **voiceless** and **voiced**.

📖 Pronounce the "**voiceless th**" sound by lightly sticking your tongue BEHIND your top teeth and blowing a little air as in "*Thank you*." Put your fingers under your jaw line as you say the "breath th". There is NO vibration as you say, "Thank you." ☆ **Thank you.**

☆ **thank**
thick
thank
thorn
thumb
threat

thaw
three
thirteen
thirty
thistle

bath
thread
wreath
broth
mouth
thrifty
athlete

author
Arthur
pathway
faithful
cloth ✏️

📖 The "**voiced th**" sound is a bit different. Use your vocal cords. Blow and vibrate or *quiver* your tongue slightly. If you place your fingers just under your jaw line, you should feel a vibration. The *voiced th* is in these words:

this   **that**
those **the**
these **then**
there **thus** ✏️

A Bit of PH History!

Do not get caught in the ph /f/ typhoon. The ph probably started thousands of years ago with the languages of the Greeks and Romans. We can blame them for our troubles. These words are not difficult to read. Read across any big word, one sound at a time!

Remember: ph = /f/

☆ phantom
phase
phrase
phen·om·en·al

Ralph
nephew
phī·al
phlegm

phosphorus
phlox
photographer
photography
Phillip

phil·an·thro·py
āphid
typhoon
pharynx
amphibian

phōtōstat
Phoēnix
gōpher
Jōseph
soph·o·mōre

naphtha
diphtheria
orphan
dolphin
sap·phire
Phew!

📖 **But wait!** Can you read a bonus word?
The c at the end says /k/.

☆phil·har·mon·ic

WORDS WITH WH CAN BE A PROBLEM!

Notice words that begin with w when you read. Notice if they begin with the w as /w/ as in *wagon* or the /wh/ breath sound as in *what*.

The words in the lists on this page begin with a slight wh *breath* sound. If you put your finger in front of your mouth and blow slightly as you say "**wh**uh," you should feel a small puff of air.

HAVING TROUBLE? Historically, the wh may have been spelled and spoken as hw, not wh. Reverse the sounds. Say /hw/. Now, do you notice the puff.

☆ whale
wharf
what
wheat

wheel
wheeze
wheedle
whelm

whatever
when
where

☆ **whether**
whetstone
whet [Not the same as *wet*.]
whew
whey™ /whā/
which
whichever
whiff
whiffle
Whig Party
while
whim

whimper
whimsy
whine
whiny
whinny
whippersnapper
whirr
whirl
whirlwind
whisker
whip
whiz
whisk

Chapter 5 Review

📖 I will read the question. You provide the answer.

1. When we refer to digraphs, we mean we use two _____ to write one _ _____ .

2. When a <u>ch</u> sound follows a short vowel, you MUST have a "_____".

3. True or False? Long vowel teams require a blocker before ch. _____

4. For words beginning with <u>wr</u>, which letter is silent? _____

5. The <u>ph</u> in English words says /___/.

6. Which of the following letter combinations are not digraphs: <u>th</u>, <u>wh</u>, <u>bl</u>, <u>sh</u>, <u>str</u>, <u>ch</u>? _____ _____

7. Some words that begin with <u>wh</u> once may have been spelled with _____, not <u>wh</u>.

Answers: 1. letters/sound 2. blocker 3. False 4. w 5. /f/ 6. bl/str 7. hw

Chapter 6

Confusing Concepts That Follow Rules — Most of the Time!

📖 ILD, IGN, IND, GH AND OTHERS

The concepts on the next few pages may seem to be a bit confusing. They include how to read and spell words containing *old spellings* with *new pronunciations or old pronunciations* with *new spellings*.

They are groups that try to confuse!

The i looks like it should be pronounced as a *short* vowel, but is pronounced as a *long* vowel.

The g and gh noticeably were pronounced over 1500 years ago, but not now!

You will learn more in these next lessons. Practice helps!

Say i as in time.

☆ **wild**
mild
child 📝

Say i as in time.
The g is silent.

☆ **si̶g̶n**
desi̶g̶n *
resi̶g̶n * 📝

Say i as in time.

☆ **find**
remind
grind
kind
blind
binder
wind
behind
bind 📝

---

* 📖 Here is an example of how one word may have various pronunciations.. The word is *design*. You may hear people say
dē-zi̶g̶n, dezign, dizign or *duhzign*.

📖 **HERE ARE MORE OLD SOUNDS AND SPELLINGS THAT DO NOT HAVE TO BE CONFUSING. PRACTICE!**

📖 **īgh**

Say the i as in ice
The g and h are silent.
Hundreds of years ago, they were pronounced.

☆ **si~~gh~~**
mi~~gh~~t
li~~gh~~ten
hi~~gh~~
bri~~gh~~ten
ti~~gh~~t
ti~~gh~~ten
ri~~gh~~t
ni~~gh~~t
mi~~gh~~ty

spri g h tly
sli g h t
fli g h t
bri g h t
si g h

📖 A few words like ***chīld*** and ***chĭldren*** or ***wīnd*** and ***wĭnd*** can be a challenge.
Context clues help with pronunciation.

📖+☆ The chīld may help to wīnd some of the old clocks.

T See * note about (').

📖+☆ The chĭldren saw the boat's flag blowing in the gentle wind that is a light breeze.

* 📖 The mark (') in the next sentence is an *apostrophe*. The *apostrophe* s or 's means ownership or "belongs to". The apostrophe (') has no sound. Just read across the word from beginning to end as in "my friend's house".

📖 TIME FOR REVIEW

Try silly MULTI-SYLLABLE WORDS.

📖 Sometimes you will see unfamiliar words. They may be science words or names in history. Below are some silly words that will provide practice in reading long words that you have never heard before.

📖 Read from *left to right* saying each sound.
- Say the vowel name in **dark red**.
- The letter in gray is silent.
- Say the short vowel sounds in blue.
- Remember vowel teams.

☆ 1. **prēad·bēal·chēat**   3. **kwick·snick·chāy**

2. **chaistēafnew**   4. **kwaythaypain**

📖 IMPORTANT! If you are reading unfamiliar or difficult words, you can be very confident. On paper or in your mind, follow the rules. Mark the long vowels. Cross out silent vowels; identify troublemakers, etc. Change the shape of your mouth as you read each sound across the word, left to right.

> 📖 **For words with no visual aids, follow the rules.**
> **Read across.** Do not skip any sounds.

☆ 5. **stucktaystain**   9. **remindhighbail**
   6. **fleascreamraid** 10. **spealpaymain**
   7. **batbaitmanmain** 11. **mainbaitbatman**
   8. **chainnewbeen**   12. **kwackpeckpen**

📖 Spell #5 & #6. Take note of troublemakers that you must remember. 📓✏️

> 📖 **Wow! Don't look so confused. You <u>can</u> read these sentences.**

☆1. The w<u>ild</u> child was not m<u>ild</u>.

2. I f<u>ind</u> that I must rem<u>ind</u> the ch<u>ild</u> to w<u>ind</u> the clock.

3. A kind bl<u>ind</u> man went beh<u>ind</u> my window bl<u>ind</u>s to find his b<u>ind</u>er.

4. The city will design Main Street's sign.

5. I find delight when I take a flight in a bright airplane.

6. The sight of a bright light may frighten the child on the right side.

📖+☆ Did you read these words the *right* way?

📖 The **ūe**, **ūi** and **ew** say /ū/.

STUBBORN-AS-A-TRICKY-MŪLE REVIEW

The **ūe**, **ūi**, **ew** all say the letter **name** (*long sound*) **of /ū/.**

Say ui, ue, ew as /ū/ with a *moon /oo /* sound.

📖 /u**e**/ /oo/ ☆ **blue   rue   clue**
true   glue   Tuesday
Sue   sue   rescue

📖 ™ Let's review these words with exceptions.

☆ **cru·el   fu·el   du·el   gr·uel**

📖 /**ū**i/ ☆ **suit   fruit   suitable**
suitor   suited   re·cruit

📖 ew=**ū** Say the consonant sounds + /ū/. Remember that the letter w comes from old uu. Say, "Double u"! Therefore, euu became **ew**. Read ew quickly as /ēū/ or simply /ū/.

☆ **blew** /blū/   **grew**   **pew**   **chew**
few   **crew**   **flew**   **stew**
drew   **brew**   **steward**   **news**
threw   **Drew**   **renew**

📖 You must study the spelling of these words to know which ue, ui, ew to use. We will pre-analyze for this quiz because the sound over-lap can be especially confusing. A diphthong such as ew is a 2-part sound. **Diphthongs** are "**gliding vowels**" made from sliding from one vowel to another quickly within the same syllable. 📖✏

EUREKA! The eu and ew sound like u.

Remember that the Roman letter v was pronounced as /ū/. That is why we have the diphthongs eu and ew that sound alike.

For example, to say the word *few*, exaggerate as "fēuū". Slide and glide the ēuū fast. We may hear /oo/ or /ēū/.

Pronunciation varies. When in doubt, dictionaries are always helpful.

1. **dew**	21. **feudal**	**Bonus Tip**
2. **spew**	22. **neuron**	☆+
3. **aircrew**	23. **strewn**	**pneumonia**
4. **view** (vēū)	24. **dewdrop**	
5. **chew**	25. **strew**	
6. **Lewis**	26. **eschew**	Ask students if
7. **grew**	27. **askew**	there are words
8. **neutral**	28. **new**	whose meanings are unfamiliar.
9. **ewer**	29. **Europe**	
10. **mew**	30. **eulogy**	Give some of the meanings. Look up
11. **deuce**	31. **feud**	some words.
12. **Teutonic**	32. **stew**	
13. **amateur**	33. **hew**	Make this a fast and fun activity.
14. **drew**	34. **euphony**	
15. **mildew**	35. **lieu** (lēū)	Dictionary work is
16. **curfew**	36. **Newton**	like detective work, solving a mystery
17. **crew**	37. **vacuum**	of unknown words.
18. **pew**	38. **steward**	
19. **grew**	39. **anew**	
20. **chewable**	40. **EUREKA!**	

📖 **Sometimes you will meet nice people with silly names. Sometimes you will meet silly people with silly names.**
READ THE SOUNDS. FOLLOW THE RULES!

When in doubt, ask politely, "How do you pronounce your name?"

☆ 1. **I know Mr. Cheapfeat.**
2. **We saw Sam Stewseal.**

> 📖 This next name could be pronounced with a long i – Mildpeat. It could also be pronounced with a short i, as in Mildpeat.
> Names can have different or unusual pronunciations.

☆ 3. **Give a box to Mrs. Mildpeat.**

> 📖 The author of PSRS pronounces her last name as DŌ-**RAŃ** with the accent on the last syllable. People with the same spelling may pronounce it **DŌŔ**–AN. This is a personal choice. You may ask politely, "May I ask how you pronounce your name?" That is courteous and acceptable.

☆ 4. **That man is Quint Weaksqueak.**
5. **Call Mr. or Mrs. Trainerdrainer.**
6. **Open doors for Mr. Pewterpan.**
7. **Sit with Mr. or Mrs. Bruelpaint.**
8. **Look for Sue Pightmight.**
9. **Sell candy to Lewis Strewslue.**

[T] Analyze the spelling of the names in one sentence and dictate the sentence.

The problem with spelling OW! OUCH!

That hurts! Remember: ow/ou are the "hurt sounds."

Spill coffee and you will say "Ow! Ow! Ow! Ow!"

☆bow	cowl	drowsy	dowry	vowel
wow	flower	cower	brown	power
howl	vow	meow	crowd	now

Warning! The <u>ow</u> may say the name of <u>O</u>, as in sō and nō. How will you know? You may need context clues or the dictionary to know!

| ☆ sn<u>ow</u> | tow | bow | flow | throw |
| bl<u>ow</u> | stow | crow | glow | grow |

Ou as in *ouch*.

☆

loud	about	house	found
ouch	slouch	around	dou~~b~~t ™ *
pout	flour	sour	
mouth	sound	abound	

*This word keeps <u>b</u> from its origin Latin, *du<u>b</u>ius*. Today, the <u>b</u> is not pronounced. Read as /**dout**/, but spell <u>d o u b t</u>.

Words with **−us** at the end are usually **nouns**, such as *circus*. Words with **−ous** at the end usually are **adjectives**.

-OUS AT THE END OF A WORD JUST SAYS "us". ☆

| fa·mous | ri·dic·ū·lous | mi·rac·ū·lous |
| fab·ū·lous | in·stan·tā·nē·ous | dis·as·trous |

 PRACTICAL PRACTICE

Here are a few truly nonsensical sentences to give you practice in reading words with ou/ow. Read the ou/ow sounds that usually **make the "hurt" sounds. "Ow! Ouch! That hurts!"**

1. How is the brown cow now?
2. We tried to surround the couch and shout in the house to chase the owl.
3. We used a brown vowel "A" when we made the crown for the fabulous townhouse tower.
4. A crowd in the town saw the cloud in the shape of a flower. It seems that the crowd in the town was not very busy!
5. When the couch fell on the snout of Arthur's talking pig, the pig shouted, "Ouch!" and ran.
6. The town cow can "wow" the crowd. It is a problem. The town cow just sits on the couch in the house. This town needs its own TV shōw.

Meet the -gh team.

Before 1150 A.D., these Old English sounds -gh were said a bit like gargling or clearing the throat as "hard" /g/ /h/.

Now, -gh at the end of a word says /f/.

📖 + ☆ or ☆   r o ŭ g h /ruf/

☆ The road was not smooth. It was rough.

📖 + ☆ or ☆   t o ŭ g h /tu/

☆ If something is difficult to do, we may say that "Something is tough."

📖 + ☆ or ☆   e n o u g h /enuf/

☆ At the party, we did not have too much or too little food. We had just enough.

📖 + ☆ or ☆   t r o u g h /trawf/

☆ The animals ate from the cattle trough. It is a long slender open container that we use to hold food or water for animals.

📖 + ☆ or ☆   c o u g h /kawf/

☆ I am sick with a bad cough.

📖 + ☆ or ☆   l a u g h /laf/ *

☆ It was so funny, we had to laugh.
Say "**laf**" or "**lauf**" as local or regional dialects dictate.

-gh Rules

📖 Each part into which a word is divided naturally, when it is pronounced, is called a **syllable**. The **-gh at the end of a syllable** says **/f/**, as in *cough·ing*.
We will learn more about syllables later.

☆ la~~ugh~~•able

It was laughable when the monkeys began to imitate us.

📖 Don't worry about words with **–gh + t**.

Leave **-gh** **OUT** when you **READ**.
Put **–gh** **IN** when you **SPELL**.

Say /aw/: a~~ugh~~t/o~~ugh~~t.

📖 1. **ought**:	Say /awt/	as in	☆ **bought**.
📖 2. **aught**:	Say /awt/	as in	☆ **taught**.
📖 3. **īght**:	Say /īte/	as in	☆ **night**.
📖 4. **eigh**:	Say /ā/	as in	☆ **eight** (8)

☆ ri~~gh~~t	ought	nought	straight
pli~~gh~~t	bought	naught	flight
might	fought		weight
sight	sought	📖 *Nought* and *naught* have the same meaning. *Naught* is used more commonly today.	freight
light	fraught		📖 TROUBLE-MAKER!  he~~i~~ght
tight	Dwight		📖 **Say the sounds as you write**. 📖✏

📖 Hear **aw / au** in **al**t, **au**ght, **all**, **ou**ght, as in sm**all** and t**all**. **"Alk"** sounds like **"awk."**

☆**all**	**walk**	**halt**	**call**	**hall**
gall	**wall**	**talk**	**fault**	**fall**
pall	**stall**	**mall**	**stalk**	**Walt**
malt	**ball**	**aloof**	**tall**	**calk**

📖 Some other <u>al</u> words are: ☆ **always   also   altogether   althō~~ugh~~   almi~~gh~~ty**

📖 I will dictate one sentence for spelling after you read all five.

☆ 1. We can all meet in the hall after class.

2. Halt! Stop! You cannot walk through the stalks of corn. The stalks are too tall. You may get lost.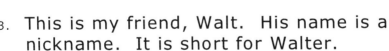

3. This is my friend, Walt. His name is a nickname. It is short for Walter.

4. Today, I will take a walk with Walt and talk.

5. He will not balk at homework. He likes to do it. 📝

PRACTICAL Reading PRACTICE

📖 1. **DON'T RISK TROUBLE.**

☆ Fill your pastime with interests and endeavors so that you or your friends can still have fun, joke, stay healthy and keep out of trouble.

A wise person never will open the door that will lead to trouble. A foolish person always does.

📖 2. **GOSSIP IS LIKE A DESTRUCTIVE FIRE.**

☆ Gossip doesn't care what kind of fuel it has provided that the wind continues to spread it.

A wise person doesn't fuel gossip, doesn't spread gossip and wants no part in the injury or destruction of another.

📖 3. **IT USUALLY TAKES MORE COURAGE TO "WALK AWAY" THAN TO "STAY AND FIGHT".**

☆ A foolish person can get into fight when he or she is controlled by emotions or by the temper of another foolish person who also has no self-control. Consider what happens if a foolish person calls you names and you answer with anger. What does that make to you? Would you be foolish times two?

A wise person considers the foolishness of the situation and walks away. It is wise to stay in control of your emotions.

Chapter 6 Review

📖 I will read the question. You provide the answer.

1. In <u>ild</u>, <u>igh</u>, <u>ign</u>, and <u>ind,</u> the <u>i</u> looks like it should be said a *short* ĭ, but it is pronounced as _____.

2. When we see <u>ue</u>, <u>ui</u> and <u>ew</u>, we generally pronounce them as the letter name of _____.

3. What rules must you follow when you have to read unfamiliar names? _____.

4. If you are having trouble pronouncing a name, what is a polite question you may ask? _____

5. How is -<u>ous</u> at the end of a word pronounced?

6. Pronounce these words: ☆   n<u>au</u>ght b<u>ou</u>ght

7. A -<u>gh</u> at the end of a word says _____.

---

1. the name of I (long i)   2. u   3. The phonics rules   4. When in doubt, ask politely. "How do you pronounce your name?"   5. /us/   6. / aw/ /aw/   7. / f/

Chapter 7

Practical Strategies to Conquer Common Reading Challenges Like C, G, –TED/-DED AND FRIENDS

📖 What sound does this letter make?

T: Student answer is optional.

📖 **Answer: You may not know.
It depends on the letter that follows it.**

📖 HERE IS THE LETTER C.

Most people do not know that they cannot tell what sound to make when they read <u>C</u>, until they know the letter that follows it!

> 📖 When you are reading a word and come to a <u>C</u>, **quickly notice the very next letter**.
> When you see <u>ce</u>, <u>ci</u> or <u>cy</u>, pronounce **c** as /S/.

☆**<u>c</u>ent** <u>c</u>enter century cinnamon citizen incite recital cement cymbal cellar	central censor silence li<u>c</u>en<u>s</u>e in<u>c</u>en<u>s</u>e* placid spice fleece tacit	vicinity Cicero certain ™** ☆ I am certain that Cicero was a wise Roman citizen who died in the year 43 B.C. ***

*📖 Spell correctly. Analyze: *li<u>c</u>en<u>s</u>e and in<u>c</u>en<u>s</u>e*.
📖 **READ: SAY ser-tᵊn. **SPELL:** Exaggerate and say cert*ai*n.
***📖 **B.C.** means the number of years **before the birth of Christ**.
B.C.E. also may be used, meaning **"Before Common Era"**.
Therefore, we also could say Cicero died in 43 B.C.E.

Cartoon candy cane!

> 📖 *If a c is followed by any other letter except e, i, y,*
>
> *—it says the /k/ sound.*
>
> You have already learned the other exception: ch on p. 92.

☆
cash	cuff	optical	cannot
collar	scurry	concrete	cape
because	coast	coffee	critical
concede	conclude	castle™	vacuum™*

*📖 To spell *vacuum* correctly, exaggerate **vac·u·um**.

📖 **If C is the LAST LETTER in a word, say /k/.**

☆ picnic   Pacific   specific   Atlantic 📝

📖 **TRY YOUR "C" SKILLS WITH THESE SENTENCES.**

☆ 1. We can scurry and have time for a cup of coffee.

2. I concede that, because you are in this class, you are a confident reader.

3. My compact car got stuck in wet concrete.

4. In October, we went to visit a specific castle replica near the Pacific Coast. ✏ Optional.

📖 This page tests to "c" how well you know the rules for c.

This page may be reproduced. Students also may write the answers on a separate paper or in their spelling journal.

📖 **For each word, write s or k for the sound of c in the word.** Do not read words. Just write the sound of each c. Further directions for reading and spelling are on next page.

1. **canvas** _____
2. **canoe**™ _____
3. **notice** _____
4. **concordance** _/_/_
5. **conference** _/_
6. **evacūate**™ _____
7. **arctic** _/_
8. **bacteria** _____
9. **cupid** _____
10. **curb** _____
11. **picnic** _/_
12. **cream** _____
13. **license** _____
14. **celebrity** _____
15. **ecstatic** _/_
16. **acre** _____
17. **citadel** _____
18. **crescent** _/_
19. **crocodile** _/_
20. **pacify** _____

📖 Compare and correct your answers with those on the next page.

> ANSWER KEY FOR PAGE 120.

📖 **This page lets you know how well you know the c-rules and can read words with c.**

☆ Correct your answers and then read the words.

1. **canvas**_k_
2. **canoe**™ _k_
3. **notice**_s_
4. **concordance**_k/k/s_
5. **conference** _k/s_
6. **evacuate** _k_
7. **arctic**_k/k_
8. **bacteria** _k_
9. **cupid**_k_
10. **curb**_k_

11. **picnic**_k / k_
12. **cream**_k_
13. **license** _s_
14. **celebrity**_s_
15. **ecstatic** _k / k_
16. **ācre**™_k_
17. **citadel**_s_
18. **crescent**_k/s_
19. **crocodile** _k/k_
20. **pacify**_s_

📖 How many did you get correct? Could you have done this well before you began this course? Now, read the words.

This is a good page to review for spelling practice.

Pre-study the words. Identify troublemakers. Take note of the placement of c and s in *license*. Many people reverse them. Study and remember to know when to use one letter rather than another. As always, if you make errors, LEARN FROM YOUR MISTAKES. 📝

📖 When you have two c's together, follow the C RULES.

1. The first c has the sound of /k/. That is because it is NOT followed by e, i, or y. It is followed by c.

2. Then, look to see what letter follows the second c. Follow C's rule for the second c. (Consider each c separately.) The second c may have either an /s/ or /k/ sound.

The word **ac c e nt** is pronounced **ak·sent**.
↓ ↓
k s

Pronounce the following words. If c is followed by c, then the first c **always** says /k/. The second c follows the rules for ce, ci, or cy.

☆ accent	access	occipital
acceptance	eccentric	accept
accession	accident	accomplish
accelerate	accessible	successe 📝

☆ The eccentric man had an accident because the car's phone accessory was not accessible. He looked under the seat while he was driving. He had pushed the accelerator before he assessed the situation. 📖 What do you think happened?

📖 Note: The words **as·sess** and **ac·cess** are different.
☆ He will access the report and assess the situation.

What sound does this letter make?

T: Student answer is optional

Answer:
It depends on the letter that follows it.

What sound does a make?

> **What sound does a G make – not what sound does a *giraffe* make!**
> Most people do not know that the g has special rules! To know what sound the g should be, look at the letter that comes **after** g.
>
> The rule for ge, gi, gy is not as regular as that of ce, ci, cy. Usually, ge, gi, gy, g says /j/. However, g may "break the rule".

A Bit of History: Spelling Adaptations

T READ OR EXPLAIN:

In 1017 A.D., the King of Denmark took over the throne of England and for the next 25 years, Danish kings ruled England. Now, more than 1,400 places in England have Danish names like Der*by*, Rug*by*, Grims*by* (*–by*, a town) and Al*thorp* and Lin*thorpe* (*–thorpe,* a village).

The letter g mixed with other languages--even other letters--around this time.

The language was *fluid*, like water, flowing out in different ways and taking different forms, adjusting, *fitting in*. Spellings and pronunciations were not regular. **The English writer, Chaucer, often wrote *yive* for the word *give*.**

Influences of the many people from Scandinavian (Danish) tribes caused changes when common people lived and worked together with the Anglo-Saxons (the people from the lands of England.) Today, languages *adopt* new words. Margaret M. Bryant, Modern English and Its Heritage, Macmillan Company, NY, 1962.

However, SOMETIMES ge *and* gi have the 'hard' sound of g as in *go*. Because of changes over time, a FEW exceptions do not follow the g-rule such as the following words: give, gift, giver, given, begin, girl, fish gill, and target.

GET GOOD AT READING A G THAT SAYS /j/

📖 **ge** /j/

☆ refūgee
gesture
gentleman
sug**g**est
dānger

gentle
generate
germ
cāgey
fringe→
Germany
angel

📖 Explain how these words are different:
☆ angel angle

📖 **gi** /j/
☆ perigee
gist
magic

ge/gi/gy

margin
origin
charging
fūgitive
dirigible

gigantic
ginger

perigee
tragic
longitude
original
eligible

📖 Remember: ia and iu say /ē/ /uh/.

☆ Alger**ia**
Belg**iu**m

📖 **gy** /j/
☆ gym
gypsy

apogee
lethargy
stingy
edgy
prodigy

📖 Let's review troublemakers in words, for example, note the d in -edge.

☆	midget
gadget	fidget
hedge	wedge
sludge	badge
ledge	📓✏

📖 If you have a base (or root) word ending in "hard" g like *bug*, and you want to add a y at the end, you must double the g. Still pronounce only the hard g sound of *bug*.

The second g does not follow the gy rule and is silent. If *fog* is the root word, how is this pronounced?
☆   foggy

📖 Review of G Words.
Golly Gee!!

📖 Check the line next to the words that have the /j/ sound of the letter g. If you are using another paper, write the numbers 1-50. Next to each number, write a g or a j to indicate the specific sound g in the word. This page may be duplicated.

✏️ Correct the answers with the students. Remind them that a wise person learns from his or her mistakes and improves in the future. Then, have the students read the words.

1.	gender____	26.	magnet____
2.	goose____	27.	wedge____
3.	gas____	28.	August____
4.	gentle____	29.	codger____
5.	grand____	30.	group____
6.	generate____	31.	George____
7.	glass____	32.	ginger____
8.	gem____	33.	giraffe____
9.	graft____	34.	gelatin____
10.	grass____	35.	regular____
11.	gutter____	36.	vagabond____
12.	genuine____	37.	segment____
13.	grit____	38.	manage____
14.	glory____	39.	gravity____
15.	grimace____	40.	German____
16.	gold____	41.	agent____
17.	grip____	42.	longitude____
18.	great™____	43.	legislate____
19.	grime____	44.	vegetable____
20.	game____	45.	pigeon____
21.	gallon____	46.	emerge____
22.	engage____	47.	pygmy____
23.	garage____	48.	insurgent____
24.	vagrant____	49.	courage____
25.	wagon____	50.	bandage____

Answer Key for Page 126.

Golly Gee!

Correct the papers with the students. Remind them that a wise person learns from his or her mistakes and improves in the future. Then, have students read the words.

1. **ge**nder J
2. **g**oose G
3. **g**as G
4. **ge**ntle J
5. **g**rand G
6. **ge**nerate J
7. **g**lass G
8. **ge**m J
9. **g**raft G
10. **g**rass G
11. **g**utter G
12. **ge**nuine J
13. **g**rit G
14. **g**lory G
15. **g**rimace G
16. **g**old G
17. **g**rip G
18. **g**reat ™G
19. **g**rime G
20. **g**ame G
21. **g**allon G
22. en**ga**ge G/J
23. **ga**rage G/J
24. va**g**rant G
25. wa**g**on G
26. ma**gn**et G
27. wed**ge** J
28. Au**gu**st G
29. cod**ge**r J
30. **g**roup G
31. **Ge**or**ge** J/J
32. **gi**n**ge**r J/J
33. **gi**raffe J
34. **ge**latin J
35. re**gu**lar G
36. va**ga**bond G
37. se**gm**ent G
38. mana**ge** J
39. **g**ravity G
40. **Ge**rman J
41. a**ge**nt J
42. lon**gi**tude J
43. le**gi**slate J
44. ve**ge**table J
45. pi**ge**on J
46. emer**ge** J
47. py**g**my G
48. insur**ge**nt J
49. coura**ge** J
50. banda**ge** J

correct ___

A Bit of History: The -ng Family

📖 The short vowel + <u>n</u> + throat <u>g</u> slide together, as though you are swallowing. The <u>-ng</u> sound is not a hard "guh" sound because /n/ slides into /g/ and softens it.

HERE IS A LITTLE BACKGROUND HISTORY TO HELP YOU TO UNDERSTAND
As ordinary people in tribes got together, they picked up words from each other. Old English, Germanic, Greek, French and Latin words were used as folks met to socialize or conduct business. To expand meanings, people adapted their words with word parts of other people they met. The *-ang, -eng, -ing, -ong*, and *-ung* is an example. *Furlong* comes from people talking about the *length of a furrow*. Also, people may have substituted an <u>–ng</u> sound for <u>–nk.</u>   Modern English and Its Heritage, p.157.

☆ **bang**
clang
rang
sang
length
strength
strengthen
bring
wing
winging
sling
singing

fling
flinging
jingle
flamingo
ring
string
kingdom
gong
belong
strong
lung
congress
tangle

finger
stinger
tongue
angle

For words <u>starting</u> with <u>gn</u> and <u>kn</u>, the /g/ and /k/ were once pronounced. Now, they are silent.
☆ gnome   gnat
   gnaw   knee
   knack   knap
   knead

📖 Practice: ☆ Please place a toy with a <u>bang</u>, a <u>ping</u>-<u>pong</u> paddle, a <u>gong</u>, a rock<u>ing</u> horse and seven r<u>ings</u> into a long, strong sack.

Trouble-Making Pretenders: Sounds of /sh/, /szh/

A Bit of History: Spelling Adaptations

Some sounds and/or spellings have evolved. We may hear sounds pronounced as though they are written as <u>sh</u> or <u>zsh</u>. They may have been written as part of the word at one time, but are not any longer. Perhaps people just slurred these sounds as they spoke.

They wrote letters to make sounds as they heard them. Sometimes, our Standard English spellings reflect the influence of spelling of other languages. Students may mark the troublemakers before they read.

| Use a dictionary as needed.

 ☆az**ure**
 plea**sure**
 trea**sure**
 colli**si**on <br> vi**si**on <br> expo**sure**
 compo**sure**
 mea**sure**
 deci**si**on <br> revi**si**on | **osier**
 hosiery
 glāzier

 📖 The next two words are pronounced the same. Both words mean a *container to hold charcoal, fire.*

 ☆
 brā'sier
 brā'zier*
 (brā-*zsh*ure)

  | **seizure**
 (see-*zsh* ure)

 leisure
 (lee-*zsh* ure)

 📖 When you see these words, pay attention to *troublemaking pretenders* so that you will spell them correctly.

 📋 Spelling analysis is **necessary** for this lesson. **Pre- view and pre- analyze words to be spelled.** Give 2-3 words at a time. Use a dictionary as needed. |

"Sh" Pretender Teams:
/-tion/ /-sion/ /-cial/ /-sial/ /-tial/ /-tious/ /-cious/

As we have seen, language and pronunciation change over the years. We write the letters, but we often *slur* their sounds when we speak. We slide them so fast that the sound seems to change. Try saying the sounds, /t/ /ee/ /on/ quickly fifteen times. Can you hear the slur? If you go very fast, it sounds something like *"shun."* "Sh" TEAMS WITH /-tion/ /-sion/ and /-cial/ /-sial/ /-tial/ /-tious/ /-cious/.

THIS WHOLE TEAM BREAKS THE RULES!
If a -ti, -ci, or -si is followed by a vowel, it usually says /sh/:

op-tion = op-/shun/

pa-tient = pā-/shent/   cau-tious = cau-/shus/

When an a or o comes just before any -tion/-sion team member, an a or o usually says its name: nā-tion or nō-tion.

☆ **fiction** fik·shun
addition add·i·shun
mul·ti·pli·cā·tion
division
nominā·tion
ac·cū·mū·lā·tion
par·tial
substan·tial
residen·tial
explō·sion

infectious
repe·ti·tious
ambitious
delicious
nutritious
vorācious
conscious
uncon·cious
fictitious
vicious 📄✏ *

* 📖📄✏ Learn which words are spelled with si or ti or ci: /sh/-sounding troublemakers. Pay special attention to the silent o when spelling –ous.

📖 MORE -_TIONS_ IN 🏃 MO_TION_!

Follow the rules that you have learned. You will probably make some _accommodation_ (change) for your local _dialect_ (accent). The **a** before –tion says its name.
USE CONTEXT TO UNDERSTAND THE MEANING OR USE A DICTIONARY.

☆ **add·i·tion   nom·i·nā·tion   con·ven·tion**

There was an addition to the nomination list at the convention to elect a president.

si·tu·ā·tion   for·mā·tion   con·sid·er·ā·tion

After careful consideration, there was a formation of a group to study the situation.

sen·sā·tion   fū·mi·gā·tion   ac·com·mo·dā·tion

Because of the fumigation in the hotel to kill large insects, the burning chemical sensation made the people sick. The hotel made other accommodations.

e·vap·or·ā·tion   prē·scrip·tion   spec·u·lā·tion

There was speculation that the evaporation of some of the medicine made the prescription too weak to be effective.

📖 You may hear some people incorrectly say "**per**scription". The correct pronunciation is **_prescription_**. Pre is a prefix or word part added on at the beginning of some words to add to or change their meanings. **Pre** means _before_. **Script** means _to write_. Therefore, a doctor **WRITES** a _pre_-scription **BEFORE** the patient can get medication. You will learn more about prefixes in PSRS.

📄✏ 3-5 words.

> **ALL IN THE FAMILY PLAY ON THE SAME TROUBLE-MAKING TEAM: -tient, -cient!** They sound like /shent/.

- Read **ti** or **ci** as though they were written /sh/.
- Read -**ti**ent as /-shent/ ☆ -**ti**ent
- Read -**ci**ent as /-shent/ ☆ effi**ci**ent.
- Learn which /shent/ending begins with **ci** as in /–cient/ and which begins with **ti** as in /-tient/ for spelling accuracy.

☆ 1. **patient**   My doctor took care of his **patient**.
  2. **ancient**™ **Ancient** history tells about events from thousands of years ago.
  3. **deficient** My new, **deficient** TV didn't work.
  4. **sufficient** My $4.00 was not **sufficient** to buy a $5.00 book.
     My $4.00 was **insufficient** to buy a $5.00 book.

> **Review other members of the -*ti*™ team.**
> These are written –**tial**, -**sial**, -**cial** but pronounced /shal/.

☆ 5. **partial:** The order was incomplete, a **partial** order.

  6. **confidential:** He could not see the **confidential** report.

  7. **martial:** The words **martial** and marital are different.

  8. **facial:** He looked at Joy's happy **facial** expression.

  9. **palatial:** The house was **palatial**, like a palace.

 10. **glacial**: **Glacial** movement is a slow-moving ice river.

 11. **nuptial:** A **nuptial** song was sung at the wedding.

 12. **residential:** Ann's house is on a **residential** street.

📖 **SYLLABICATION RULES!** There are often exceptions. Assume that these rules include the word "usually!" We know by now that there are always exceptions in English!! When in doubt, use a dictionary.

On this page and the next, I will read the rule. You will read the words.

📖 1. Every syllable has one vowel sound.

📖 2. The number of vowel sounds in a word = the number of syllables.
☆ sit = 1   hap·py = 2   bas·ket·ball = 3

📖 3. A one-syllable word is not divided.
☆ hat   stop   swish

📖 4. Consonant blends, diphthongs, and digraphs are never divided.
☆ bleach·ing   swish·ing   hun·dreds

📖 5. When a word has a <u>ck</u> or <u>x</u>, divide after <u>ck</u> or <u>x</u>.
☆ ex·it   tax·i   nick·el

📖 6. A compound word is divided between two words.
☆ with·out   tooth·brush   base·ball

> 7. When two or more consonants [c] come between two vowels [v], usually divide between the two consonants: cv·vc.
>   ☆ **an·gry   mis·ter   muf·fin**

> 8. When a single consonant comes between two vowels in a word, usually divide after the consonant if the vowel is "short": vc·v.
>   ☆ **clev·er   cab·in   lev·el**

> 9. When two vowels come together in a word are **sounded separately,** divide the word between vowels.
>   ☆ **di·et   cre·ate   ra·di·o**

> 10. Prefixes and suffixes are separate syllables. An <u>a</u> or <u>o</u> before a suffix, usually says its own name.
>   ☆ **nā·tion   rā·cial   lō·tion**

> There are other rules for syllabication. You can learn more on your own. When in doubt, use a dictionary.

CAREFUL PRACTICE MAKES ~~PERFICT~~ ~~PERFICE~~ ~~PREFICT~~ PERFECT!

- Read these. **Note the troublemakers.**
- All of the words here are separated into syllables, as found in a dictionary to aid with correct pronunciation.
- Read and spell the sounds across left to right.

☆ con·ven·tion
con·sid·er·a·tion
temp·ta·tion
im·po·si·tion

> In the next word, remember to clearly pronounce the g when you read and spell.

☆ rec·og·ni·tion
sit·u·a·tion
reg·u·la·tion
spec·u·la·tion
e·val·u·a·tion
sim·u·la·tion

par·ti·ci·pa·tion
me·di·a·tion
med·i·ta·tion
su·per·sti·tion
suc·ces·sion
in·ci·sion
e·vap·or·a·tion
ver·sion
pro·vi·sion
sub·mer·sion
ju·di·cial
spa·cial
of·fi·cial

ses·sion
par·tial
mar·tial
pres·i·den·tial
ev·i·den·tial
pes·ti·len·tial
com·mer·cial
ex·is·ten·tial

> In the next word, follow the rules for ge/gi/gy although the g and i are in separate syllables.

☆ leg·is·la·tion

📖 It's *not* a dip song! It's a diphthong!

A diphthong is a sound made from changing the mouth position to make one vowel sound slide into another vowel sound quickly and smoothly. Make your mouth say /Ō/. Quickly, change the shape to say /ĭ/. Hear the "one sound: /oi/.

📖 **oi**
☆ **point**
poise
broil
boil
avoid
cloister
foil
foist
hoist
joint
joist
coil
doily

moist
poinsettia

📖 Also acceptable: /point/set/tuh/.

tabloid
appoint
coin
oily
void
foil
soil→
boisterous
embroider

📖 **toy**
☆ **Troy**
Joy
joy
soy
Roy
oyster
destroy
employ
alloy
annoy
loyalty
coy 📄✏️*

📖 Most *oy* diphthongs come at the end of words, but not always.

> 📖 **YOU CAN TAKE A BITE OUT OF HARD WORDS!**
> **Read letters across the word from *left to right*.**

📖 Use a dictionary to expand your vocabulary! In a dictionary, the syllable to be stressed is indicated by a mark (') or in **bold**. Below, the syllables to be stressed are **bold**. Hint: Often, but not always, the 3rd syllable from the end is stressed.

☆

ā-e	spec**ū**lāte	in**val**idate	e**vap**orate
ēe	draf**tēe**	award**ees**	nomi**nee**
ē-e	com**pēte**	com**plete**	re**plete**
ī-e	in**vīte**	re**cite**	di**vide**
ō-e	an**te**lōpe	an**ti**dote	im**plode**
ū-e	ex**ac**titūde	**ap**titude	**sub**terfuge
-a-	b**a**ckpack	**boom**erang	fan**tas**tic
-e-	senti**men**tal	**neg**ligence	**pes**tilence
-i-	**in**nerspring	in**sen**sible	ci**vil**ity
-o-	**con**tact	on**col**ogy	**odd**ity
-u-	mist**rust**	unim**por**tant	**frus**trate
a(r)	regist**rar***	**ar**chery	**ar**thropod
aw	**aw**fully	**draw**back	**paw**paw
oo	**moon**beam	bas**soon**	**roof**er
oo	**foot**stool	**cook**book	**look**out
ow**	**cow**ard	**down**town	**flow**erpot

*📖 Not the same as *register*.
**📖 <u>Ow</u> as in *ouch*!

PRACTICAL PRACTICE

📖 **TROUBLEMAKERS** (sometimes called **SIGHT-WORDS**):

📖 **they** /thay/ ☆**They** took snacks with them.
📖 **their** /thĕr/ ☆They went to **their** favorite park.
📖 **one** /wun/ ☆They had **one** dog with them.
📖 **some** /sum/ ☆He had **some** food for the picnic.
📖 **ones** /wuns/ ☆The other dog and the cat were the **ones** they kept at home.

☆ 1. **Some people look at others with their success and say they are "lucky".** However, what that **"LUCK"** really means is that many long hours have been spent by working hard. I can be one of these "lucky" ones.

I have to ask myself if I am willing to spend the hours and to work hard to succeed.

☆ 2. **A friend is someone who helps you to be your best!** If the people that you call "friends" don't help you to be your **best,** then they aren't **real** friends. They are just people you know.

☆ 3. **If you lie down with the dogs, you will wake up with their fleas."** Those "fleas" are the troubles of fools that will cause you problems, too. Hang around with fools and the "fleas" are impossible to avoid.

STICKY – *TED* / *-DED*

📖 **When is the final -ed not a syllable?**
Stick to the *–ted/-ded* rules.
Do not come un-glued when you read or write verbs that end in **-ed**.

📖 This addition, in fact, really cannot be called a syllable. *Sometimes* it is added to words. *Sometimes* it "blends in" with what goes before it.

> 1. If –ed follows the letters **t** or **d**, pronounce it as /-ted/ or /-ded/. It is a separate ending.
> For example: *plan**ted**, fit**ted**, rai**ded**, han**ded***.

> 2. If –ed follows any other letter, the **e** is ~~silent~~.
> The ending says /**t**/ or /**d**/. For example, when you see *harmed*, say /**harmd**/. When you see *ripped*, say /**ripd**/. When you see *hopped*, say /**hopd**/.*

* 📖 The **d** may <u>sound</u> like a /t/. Local or regional dialects may differ. Exaggerate **d**'s sound /d/ when you pronounce **rippe̶d** and **hoppe̶d** to spell correctly.

📖 When you are writing and adding –ed, remind yourself that *–ed* acts like the **silent e** or a **y** at the end. You must double **the consonant before e or y to keep the vowel short.** If you do not want the vowel sound in the "root" word to change from short to long, you MUST double the consonant blockers.

"Yesterday, I shopped."
🚫 Do not write, "Yesterday, I shōped."

> Also, **-ing acts like a final shadow E** so you must double the consonant to keep the vowel short: sho**pp**ing *not* shōping, ti**pp**ing *not* tīping, ru**nn**ing *not* rūning.

> **PRACTICE STEPS** to follow for correct pronunciation of words with **-ed**.

1st - Underline the t's and d's **THAT COME JUST BEFORE** the final –ed.
2nd - Go down the list and pronounce those words that have -ted/-ded as final syllables.
3rd - Go back and read all of the other non -ted/-ded words.

☆ formed
coun<u>ted</u>
alter<u>ed</u>
picked
stuffed
stopped

waited
locked
faded
cashed
dented
braided
rushed
hushed
slanted

marked
bossed
cuffed
stressed
beaded
asked

depended
compelled
tramped
played
steamed
rooted
destroyed
ignored
prided

kicked
flopped
invaded
cursed
prodded
gassed

bellōwed
tramped
benefi<u>ted</u>™

📖 Do not double the t in *benefited*.

canceled

📖 In some countries such as England, it is spelled *cancelled*.

permitted

📖 Study spelling troublemakers.

PRACTICAL PRACTICE

Complete the past-tense of the verb in the space provided in each sentence below.
If the vowel sound does not change from short to long, double the final consonant.
Remember: Final -ed acts like a shadow e.

T The teacher *may* read along with the student, as needed.

1. The man *insist*____ that he had not *pass*____ a stop sign without stopping.

2. The officer *believe*____ him and *permit*____ him to continue his trip.

3. We *gas*____ up the car and *continue*____ our drive to visit a family.

4. That family had *aid*____ us when our car caught on fire when we *ask*____ for help.

5. The man *rob*____ the bank, but he was *arrest*____.

ANSWERS: 1. insisted, passed 2. believed, permitted 3. gassed, continued 4. aided 5. robbed, arrested

QU The Romans borrowed the letter Q from the Greeks!

In English spelling, q is followed by u. The qu says /kw/ as in **qu**een. Pay attention to the reading and spelling challenges. Don't panic! When in doubt, use a dictionary.

QU says /k/ in the French language. You may hear Quebec said as **kwih-bek**, but the **correct** French pronunciation commonly is /kay/-**bek** or /kē/-**bek**.

These words have the qu that is the /kw/ sound. Pay attention to the words in **bold** here. They are often misread and misspelled.

☆ quart /qwort/
queen
quick
quote
quill
quiver
square
quit
quiet /quī·et/
question
quad·ru·ped

squeeze
squeal
quaint

quality
quantity
quarrel
Iroquois
equine

questrian
quadrille
frēquent
squall
squadron
sē·quence
sō·lil·ō·quy
equip
ēqual
squelch

For the following word, remember that *quint means 5*.

☆ quintet

-quette says /ket/

☆ etiquette
crōquette

For the following words, borrowed from French, say /k/ when you see qu.

antique
briquette
catafalque
grōtesque
stat·ū·esque
brusque

 /kro·kay/
croquet

QU REVIEW *

In the sentences below, some words are misspelled. Identify each error. You may write the corrections on another paper.

1. Read the words exactly as they are written, *left to right*.
2. Pronounce correctly. Note any troublemaker sounds.
3. Say the sounds exactly as you are writing, *left to right*.

1. Sam is going to quite his job.
2. Divide the pie into three equil parts.
3. The worker only completed one task, but the quanity of her work was very high.
4. I ordered ten books, but the company sent only two. It was the wrong quality.
5. There was much noise at the picnic. No one was quit.

Correct answers and always **analyze any errors!**

1. *quit*: In the sentence above, there is a vowel team with a blocker. The word in the sentence says *quite*.
2. *equal*: Notice the <u>al</u>. It is not always pronounced exactly.
3. *quality*: This means *characteristic, value, worth,* or *condition*. Read each sound with accuracy.
4. *quantity*: This means *amount, measure, number of*.
5. *quī·et*™: In this ™word, <u>quī</u> is an "open syllable." The <u>e</u> is a short vowel. The <u>i</u> and <u>e</u> are <u>not</u> a vowel team.

[T] * Learners may need vocabulary assistance with this activity.

📖 **A Bit of History: Old English**

📖 READ OR EXPLAIN. Some early people knew only 1,000 or *fewer* words. *Old English* used simple, everyday words. As people came across other languages, words were adopted and changed. Vocabularies expanded and changed. Even the pronunciations changed.

Geoffery Chaucer, the Father of English literature, wrote **The CANTERBURY TALES,** *The Wyf of Bathe* around 1390. Below is as an example of the early English he used.* A modern version in each second line shows the changes from then to now. Read the Old English as you think it may have been pronounced.

📖 + ☆

> She was a worthy **womman al** her **lyve.**
> She was a worthy **woman all** her **life.**
>
> She **hadde** passed many **straunge streems.**
> She **had** passed many **strong streams.**
>
> To Rome she **hadde** been...
> To Rome she **had** been....

📖 Latin words came into everyday use because of the important translating work of John Wycliffe's in the 1300's. Can you find words similar to those of today?
1. ***he saith to hym***   4. ***I shall cume***
2. ***hele, helid***   5. ***centurion anseringe***
3. ***enter vnder my roof*** 6. **oonly**

---

1. said, him 2. heal, healed, 3. under 4. come 5. answering 6. only

*Modern English and Its Heritage (1962). : Bryant, Margaret M., New York: Macmillan Language: Internet Archive, p. 76, 77.

 A Bit of History: Latin

The Latin language of the Romans has influenced languages through the centuries. In the 1400s and 1500s, **law** and **science** used many Latin words.

Many French and Latin words were borrowed and had been used by many English-speaking people. Thus, English became a richer language. Other words came from the Dutch or German languages and those of other groups. These also added value to the English language. You may want to learn more about the development of English. It is an interesting topic to study.

Furthermore, while Latin is a "dead language," meaning it is not spoken as a native language any longer, the study of Latin would add to your knowledge of and ability to use English more skillfully. Latin *roots* are part of the English language and Latin is still an important language to learn. Some schools offer classes in the Latin language.

English lets people use a variety of levels of vocabularies. They can use just a simple vocabulary in a "popular style." They can be understood enough for them to "just get by" in life. **This is limiting.** On the other hand, you can become more knowledgeable and have an extensive vocabulary. You will be ready to go anywhere, to meet anyone and to do anything in life!

STRIVE FOR EXCELLENCE IN YOUR SPEECH.

It will benefit you in many ways.

What?

Y the Vowel? Yes, **y** can be the sound of /ĭ/ or **y** as in the name of the letter **i**.

📖 Sometimes **y** is a vowel between consonants. It could then sound like *short i* (igloo/in) as in this old name:

📖 +☆ **Hippolytus**

📖 Now, try more words with **y** as the short sound of **I**.

☆ **tyranny   symbol   syrup   system** 📓✏️

📖 Other times, when **y** is a vowel between consonants, it may be pronounced as long **i** (kīte) as in this old name:

📖 +☆ **Symon Stylites**

☆ **tyrant   type   typist   cypress**

📖 You may also hear people say *tyrant* or *cypress*.

📖 **BONUS:** These next words with **y** in the middle come from a Greek word which means *having to do with the mind*. The **p** makes no sound. **Y** says the **name of the letter i**. When a word begins with *psych*, **ch** is pronounced as /k/. Thus, /sīk/ is the pronunciation of *psych*.

📖 +☆   **psych** | **psych·ol·ō·gy**
        psych·ic | **psych·ō·gen·ic**

📖 I BEFORE E EXCEPT AFTER C!

When we spell, we write the i before e unless it follows a c.

LEARN: "**I before E except after C!**"

SAY IT WITH ME: 📖+☆ "**I before E except after C!**"

📖 Got it? Good!
Now, try saying it with your eyes closed!

☆ I before E except after C!
📖 The cei says /see/.

☆
cēiling   recēive   recēipt   decēive
decēit   concēive   perceive   conceit

📖 Read these sentences. Practice spelling.
LOOK UP MEANING OF UNKNOWN WORDS.

☆ A. Do you have the **receipt to** show that you paid for the **ceiling** repair?

B. I find it difficult to **conceive** of the fact that he tried to **deceive** you.

C. Did you **perceive** that the false **receipt** was a **deceitful** way of getting out of paying the bill?   📝 Dictate words and/or sentence(s).

📖 **PAY ATTENTION to a** troublemaker ie **team.**

It does **not** say /īe/.
NO! In some words, it says /iē/.

When you see the ie vowel team together in a word, it SOMETIMES -- but not always -- breaks the rules.

THE SECOND VOWEL **E** IS THE TEAM TALKER.
THE FIRST VOWEL **I** IS SILENT.

If you are not sure, try following the Team Talker Rule *or* the troublemaker way *or* use a dictionary!

☆ **piēce**	**fiēld**	**reliēf**
beliēve	**chiēf**	**belief**
piēdmont	**niēce**	**griēf**
achiēve	**achiēved**	**shriēk**
retriēve	**thiēf**	**wiēld**
achiēver	**griēve**	**siēge**
thiēvery	**liēn**	**shiēld**
griēving	**liēge** /lēj/	

📖 When there is a word ending in **y**, **change the y to i** and **add es**. This makes a word plural, *more than one*. The ies says /ēs/.

+ ☆ **baby →babies**
authority →authorities
allergy →allergies
melody→melodies
quantity→quantities

navy → navies
library→libraries*

*📖 Lib**ra**ry is often mispronounced as *li-berry*.
cry→cries

Chapter 7 Review

📖 I will read the question. You provide the answer.

1. The c in ce, ci, cy is pronounced as _____.

2. The c in ca, co, cu, ck, cr is pronounced as _____.

3. In the word *success*, how do you pronounce the first c? ____ How do you pronounce the second c? ____

4. The g in ge, gi, gy usually is pronounced as _____.

5. The g in ga, go, gu, gk, gr is pronounced as _____.

6. If –ed follows the letters t or d, it is pronounced as _____ or _____ and is a separate ending.

7. The endings -ed and -ing act like the silent e at the end of words. You must double the _____ if you want to keep the vowel *short* as in *begging, hopped*.

8. When I am spelling the word *ceiling*, I will have to remember the rule, ___ before ___ except after ___.

1. /s/   2. /k/   3. /k/ /s/   4. /j/   5. /g/   6. ted/ ded   7. consonant   8. i, e, c.

Chapter 8

Prefixes

YOU CAN READ WELL!
Count on prefixes to help you understand some big words!

- A prefix is a syllable added at the beginning of a word to modify (*change*) its meaning.
    - *Pre* means <u>before</u>.
    - A <u>*pre-fix*</u> comes <u>in front</u> of or is <u>fixed</u> onto the front.
- Many prefixes come from Latin meanings.
    - As mentioned before, the more Latin you know, the larger your vocabulary can be.
    - This section gives you some prefixes, but not all.
- Knowing the meaning of different prefixes will help you to determine the meaning of many new words.
- Try to learn the meaning of all of the prefixes in these final lessons.
    - Every time you learn a new prefix, review the old ones.
    - Practice! Practice! Drill instills!
    - Learn prefixes and your vocabulary will grow.

A NOTE ABOUT 2 TYPES OF DICTIONARIES

- ABRIDGED: a dictionary that has been shortened by some omitting terms or definitions.
Hint: Think of how **a bridge** *shortens* a trip, crossing a river, for example, instead of going the long way around.

- UNABRIDGED: a dictionary that has **not** been shortened by the omitting terms or definitions. For example, it will give origins of words, such as Latin or French and the meanings from those languages.

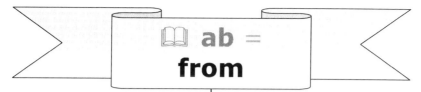

ab = from

☆ 1. abnormal
2. abstract

📖 Latin: *ab* + *trahere* = *draw*

☆ 3. abandon
4. abase

📖 Middle English *abassen*, from *a-* (from Latin *ad-*)+ *-besser*, lower

☆ 5. abrupt
📖 Latin *abruptus*, to break off

☆ 6. abduct
📖 Latin: *ab = from* Latin: *ductus = lead away*

☆ 7. abstain
8. absent

📖 Latin *absent-*, *absens* (to be away from), not present at a usual place

☆ 9. abdicate
10. absolve
11. abolish

📖 The next word, *avert* was *abvert*, but changed over the years.

☆ 12. avert
📖 From Latin *avertere*, from *ab-* + *vertere* to turn

PRACTICAL PRACTICE

☆ **Sometimes** it takes **courage** to walk away. **Absent** yourself from some group or action that may **abase** your good intentions. **Abstain** from taking part. Make decisions that will bring about the greatest good for you and for others.

Acts of cowards are **bullying, violence, gossip, cheating** or **taking what is not theirs** and any other words or actions that hurt another's possessions, body, mind or spirit. Take action to **avert** any chance to take part in the acts of cowards.

Abolish any relationships with cowards, **abruptly**, if necessary.

Courage is holding firm against what is wrong. The group may say you are "**abnormal**". However, do not **abandon** good judgment to please anyone

ad = to

★
1. adverb
2. advance
3. adhesive
4. adhere
5. advocate

6. ad·jācent
7. addition
8. advantage
9. adjust
10. ad·jective

📖 The next ten words have lost the <u>d</u> over the years. Try to say them with the <u>d</u>.

★ 11. acquire

📖 The letter after <u>a</u> has been doubled for these words.

★ 12. affix
13. aggressive
14. allude
15. annex

16. apply
17. arrest
18. assist
19. attract
20. asset

 PRACTICAL PRACTICE

★ "Ah, what a tangled web we weave when first we practice to deceive." -William Shakespeare

★ Shakespeare **alludes** to the problems that **annex** themselves to lives of those take **advantage** of a chance to lie. It is better to **admit** to the truth and resist the **attract**ion of a lie that may tangle you in troubles.

📖 ante = before

⭐ 1. antēbellum

📖 Latin: *ante = before*,
Latin: *bellicus* is *warlike*. An antebellum period was a time before war.

⭐ 2. antēcedent
3. antērior
4. antenuptial
5. antechamber
6. antepenult

7. antediluvian
8. antemeridian∗

∗ **ante** = *before*
  meridian = *middle*

📖 That is why we write **a.m.** or **A.M.** as an abbreviation for *before* the *middle* of the day. We may also write **AM** or _{AM}. Whichever way you choose, be consistent.

📖 anti = against

📖 The *i* in *anti-* is pro-nounced /ī/ or /ĭ/ depending on local or regional use. Either way is acceptable, generally. If in doubt, consult a dictionary for spelling accuracy and word meaning.

⭐ 1. antīclimax
2. antīburglar
3. antifreeze
4. antitoxin
5. antiseptic

6. antibiotic
7. an·tĭ´·pathy
8. antidote
9. antibacterial

📖 Sometimes a hyphen is used with *anti-* as in the next words:

10. antī-arthritis
11. antī-aircraft
12. antī-tax

circum = around

☆ 1. circumnavigate
2. circumlocution
3. circumspect
4. circumvent
5. circumference
6. circumscribe
7. circumstance

📖 The following words have origins related to the prefix *circum*

☆ 8. circlet
9. circus
10. circle
11. circular
12. circulate
13. circuit

PRACTICAL PRACTICE ☆

1. The arrested man affixed his name to a confession to admit that he had abducted the president's dog during the antebellum period. He was caught in the post-war time.

2. At 11 a.m., a Navy man entered the antechamber of the command room. The captain of the ship was there. He commanded the ship that was circumnavigating the world to fight against an alien enemy.

   At 3 p.m., several circular alien anti-aircraft from outer space began shooting at the world's armies and trying to abduct abnormal creatures from the circus.

📖 con

from Latin *conducere* meaning *to lead*

bring together, with

1. contract
2. congeal
3. conform
4. congest
5. congregate
6. consolidate
7. confide
8. comprehension
9. contrast
10. concur
11. concert
12. concerted

📖 The next words began the same, but the <u>n</u> has been dropped.

☆ 13. collaborate
14. correspond

📖 Generally, no hyphen is required to link this prefix to root words. In some words, like **co-operate**, you may also see it as **cooperate**. Words like **co-owner** may be confusing if written as **coowner**.

PRACTICAL PRACTICE ☆

Read all of the following directions first before doing anything.
1. Say, "It is extremely important to follow directions."
2. Say the name of your teacher.
3. In your normal speaking voice, count from five to one backwards.
4. When you reach this point, say, "It is important to follow directions."
5. Shake hands with your instructor.
6. On another paper, write your name as quickly as you can.
7. Now that you have finished reading everything, follow directions one and two only!

 **contra** =
from Latin contra meaning
against

☆ 1. contradiction
2. contraction
3. contrarian
4. contradict
5. contrary

 **dē** =
down from, reverse action

☆ 1. dēscend
2. dēhydrate
3. decompress
4. deform
5. degenerate
6. deposit
7. decrease
8. default

 PRACTICAL PRACTICE

☆ **Contrary** to what he thought would happen, Bob's pleasant manner **degenerated** into an angry attitude. Obviously, Bob's being a **contrarian** did not convince the police officer that speeding was not Bob's fault. Bob's fine for speeding that he had to pay did not **decrease**.

dis = apart, remove

☆ 1. disappear
2. disclaim
3. disobey
4. distribute

📖 Origin: From the late 16th century (originally in the sense meaning to reject a playing card): from dis- (removal) + the noun (card).

5. discard

6. discourage
7. distrust
8. dismiss
9. disagree
10. disrespect
11. discontinue
12. dishonest

📖 The s has been dropped for the following words:

☆ 13. diffuse
14. digress

 PRACTICAL PRACTICE

☆ The old man deflated the balloon after it appeared that the child discarded it and went home.

The club rule is that members will be dismissed from the club and they must depart if they show disrespect to a mentor or the rest of the students.

ex = out, out of, outside

- 1. exit
- 2. except
- 3. excel
- 4. explode
- 5. export
- 6. expel

📖 The following words may have been written with x, but the x was dropped or changed over the years.

- 7. eccentric
- 8. emerge
- 9. emigrant
- 10. effervesce
- 11. external
- 12. emigrant

📖 To *emigrate* means to go outside of a place. This means to leave.
☆ The man was an <u>em</u>igrant <u>from</u> Spain.
📖 To *immigrate* means to come into a place.
☆ He <u>im</u>migrated <u>to</u> New Zealand.

in = in, go in

- 1. invade
- 2. inhabit
- 3. insertion
- 4. induct
- 5. invest
- 6. inject
- 7. inspect
- 8. income
- 9. infection
- 10. inlay

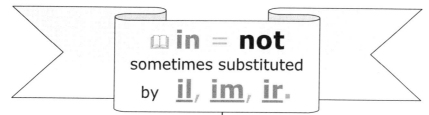

in = not sometimes substituted by **il, im, ir.**

1. invisible
2. inseparable
3. inappropriate
4. insoluble
5. indigest
6. insufficient
7. inept
8. ineligible

11. inactive
12. illegal
13. illiterate
14. immoral
15. impossible
16. immaterial
17. irresponsible
18. irreconcilable
19. irrational
20. irregular

Some words are very easy to comprehend when the prefix is added to a known or familiar word. You may have to rely on a dictionary and look up some of the words that may be unfamiliar.

 PRACTICAL PRACTICE

1. The salesman's answers to the questions were inept and irrational. The people bought the new car anyway.

2. The irresponsible company exported invisible debugging equipment. The bugs were happy!

3. You can buy very inexpensive, irregular, deflating parachutes with insufficient emergency cords on sale! Would you be interested?

inter = between,

Always use a dictionary if you are unsure of meanings, syllabication, pronunciation, or which syllable to stress.

☆
1. in·ter·act
2. in·ter·na·tion·al
3. in·ter·view
4. in·ter·vene
5. in·ter·ven·tion
6. in·ter·min·gle
7. in·ter·re·la·ted
8. in·ter·loc
9. in·ter·tri·bal
10. in·ter·weave
11. in·ter·val
12. in·ter·face
13. in·ter·change
14. in·ter·cept
15. in·ter·com

The word, *intercom*, is short for *intercommunication system*.

intra =
pronounced "intruh"
within

☆
1. intramuscular
2. intravenous
3. intracellular
4. intrastate
5. intracollegiate
6. intracardiac
7. intramundane
8. intramural

Latin: *murus* = walls, e.g. (for example), walls of a city, school

☆9. intrabox

☆
1. misinform
2. misrepresent
3. **miStaKe**

4. mismanage
5. misjudge
6. misdeal
7. mmmmisspell
8. misbehave
9. misalign
10. mistreat
11. mislead
12. misdial 📄✏️

📖 mis = wrong

📖 **THIS PREFIX PAGE HAS BEEN MISMANAGED!**

What do you think *mismanaged* means?
Can you find the mistakes?

📖 Mistakes: #3, 7, 9 and the **misplaced** title.

📖 per = through

1. percolator
2. permanent
3. persist
4. perennial
5. perspective
6. perforate
7. perspire
8. pervade
9. permē·āte
10. perforce

📖 Sometimes, we still use complete Latin phrases. *Per* is a Latin meaning **THROUGH, BY MEANS OF, FOR EVERY**....

1. *per annum* - by the year, annually
2. *per capita* - for each person
3. *per se* /say/ - considered by (or by) itself
4. *per diem* /dee-em/ - for each day, daily

---

1. Bob earned $50,000 *per annum*.
2. The business spent $3,000 *per annum*, *per capita* for insurance.
3. The mayor received $25 *per diem* for travel expenses.
4. Cars are not bad *per se*. Bad drivers cause accidents.

📖 pre = before

Remember this trick:
pre and before both end with re.

☆ 1. pretest
2. precaution
3. prescribe
4. prerequisite
5. prepossess

6. preview
7. prepare
8. precancellation
9. preamble
10. predict 📝

📖 post = after

☆ 1. postdate
2. post·hu·mous
   /pŏst hu mous/
3. postpone
4. posterity
5. post nuptial

6. postlude
7. posterior
8. post-emergency
9. post bellum
10. post date 📝

📖 Post Meridian is after the middle of the day - p.m./P.M.
Do you remember what *ante meridian* means? ☆
Meet me at 6 a.m. 📖 Is that morning or afternoon?

📖 **Post** (after)   **Script** (write)
P.S. is a note written as a thought after the signature.

pro = for, before in favor of

1. **pro**'·duce
2. proclaim
3. proceed
4. protect
5. promote
6. pro-kindness
7. profess
8. prŏspect
9. propose
10. pro·**duce**'

PRACTICAL PRACTICE

1. The wise **professor promoted pro-reading** activities.
2. Factory owners have discussion including **pro**s and cons of **producing** more **products**.
3. The man **proceeded** to write out a check to donate money to a charity project.
4. We had to **protect** the little lost puppies.
5. The **pro**duce section in the grocery store has products such as corn, beans, celery and apples that have been pro**duced** by farmers.

re = again, back

📖 ERASE AND RE-DO!

You may use a hyphen to prevent confusion in **meanings**, such as ***re-form*** and ***reform***, or **pronunciations**, such as ***re-enlist***, not ***reenlist***.

☆
1. re-do
2. retrace
3. return
4. repair
5. release

6. research
7. repeat
8. re-start
9. rēinstate
10. reprint

11. replace
12. retort
13. remīnd
14. rē·iterate

15. reply
16. refer
17. re-argue
18. report
19. reaffix
20. reabsorb

se =
aside, apart

" I selected this gift for you."

Not all words that begin with <u>se</u> have this meaning. However, the next words are words that have their origins and meanings related to <u>se</u>.

☆1. secure
2. select
3. secret
4. seclude
5. sequester

6. segregate
7. sectional
8. separate
9. secede
10. section

sub =
under, below

☆1. substitute
2. subscribe
3. submerge
4. suburb
5. sublet
6. subscript
7. submarine

8. subordinate
9. subdue
10. subaverage

 These are "sub" related words. <u>B</u> was probably left out in the following words.

11. succumb
12. support

📖 super = above, beyond

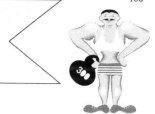

📖 **Troublemaker** alert! The **i before o** sounds like **ē** as in *superior* (*soo*-peer-**ee**-or).

☆The superior man has superhuman strength. He has super<u>ior</u> form. His nickname is *Superman*.

☆ 1. superior
2. superlative
3. superhero
4. superficial
5. supersede
6. supernatural
7. superhuman
8. superintend
9. superscript

📖 Throughout time, the Latin prefix *super* may have been shortened or changed to become *sur* as in the next two words.

☆10. <u>sur</u>pass
11. <u>sur</u>vive

📖 trans = across, through

☆ 1. transgress
2. transform
3. transit
4. transmit
5. transplant
6. translucent
7. transparent
8. translate
9. transfusion
10. transmigrate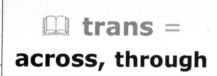

 **un = not**

 This is an <u>un</u>usual u<u>n</u>bunny.

☆ 1. unhappy
2. uncover
3. unkind
4. uncertain

5. unfortunate
6. unlucky
7. unmake
8. unload
9. unbent

📖 The following prefixes are enumerated (*numbered*) prefixes.

uni = 1

☆1. unicycle →
2. uniform
3. unicolor
4. unilateral
5. unilingual
6. unanimous
7. United States*

*📖 States united as one country.

bi = 2

☆1. bicycle →
2. bifocal

3. binocular
4. biannual
5. bilateral
6. bicolor
7. biweekly

tri = 3

☆
1. tricycle ↴
2. tripod
3. tricolor
4. triplet
5. triplicate
6. tricentennial
7. triangle 📝

📖 REVIEW of PREFIXES

You do not have to feel like a blindfolded reader and writer. Read, write, spell and comprehend accurately. Know these prefixes. We can use this page as a review.

ad- to	**ex-** out	**per-** through	**sub-** under
ante- before	**in-** in	**post-** after	**super**(sur)- above
anti- against	**in-** not	**pre-** before	**trans-** across
circum- around	**intra/intro-** within	**pro-** before, for	**un-** not
con- with	**inter-** between, among	**re-** again, back	**uni-** one
de- down, from	**mis-** wrong	**se-** aside	**bi-** two
dis- apart			**tri-** three

📖 **MORE HELPFUL PREFIXES!** These prefixes generally will be decodable for you. I will read the prefix. You will read the meaning. You and I will read the examples together, if you wish.

📖 Prefix	☆ Meaning	☆ or 📖 + ☆ Examples
1. ambi-	**both, around**	ambidextrous, ambiguity
2. amphi-	**both, around**	amphibian, amphitheater
3. auto-	**self**	autobiography, automatic
4. be -	**make**	befriend, become
5. hetero-	**different**	heteronym, heteroatom
6. meta-	**change**	metabolic, metamorphosis
7. mono-	**single, one**	monotone, monotonous
8. neo-	**new**	neonatal, neophyte
9. para-	**almost**	paralegal, paramedic
10. pseudo-	**false**	pseudonym, pseudopod

Some Prefixes SHOW *AMOUNT* or *EXTENT OF*

1. equi-	**equal**	equator, equidistant
2. hyper-	**excessive**	hyperactive, hypercritical
3. is-	**equal**	isometric, isosceles
4. multi-	**many, much**	multicolor, multi-sided
5. olig-	**few**	ol'i·go·chrome, oligopoly
6. out-	**surpass**	outbid, outclass, outlive
7. pan-	**all**	pandemonium, panacē·a
8. poly-	**many**	polychrome, polyclinic

READ AND SPELL WORDS WITH –*TURE*!

📖 The following words often have a -*ture* slur. It sounds like "chur" when the -*ture* is said fast. Say "-*ture*" rapidly. ☆ ***-ture-ture-ture-ture-ture***

📖 Read the following words but exaggerate -*ture*.
☆ **creature, nature, adventure, mature**.

📖 Note that *creature* comes from the Latin word, *cre-a- tura*. There is no slur in Latin. Because of usage over the years, the –<u>ture</u> has taken on the "chur" slur.

📖 **Slurred sounds make it difficult to spell correctly.**

Here are some tips to help you to spell –*ture* words correctly.

1. **Pronounce clearly.**
2. **<u>Exaggerate</u> the phonetic pronunciation as as in *feat – ŭre*.**
3. **Say the sounds as you write.**
4. **Remember to write the silent shadow vowels.**

As you read, always pay attention to how words are spelled.

☆ 1. picture
2. overture
3. texture
4. cincture
5. departure
6. venture
7. aperture
8. restructure
9. fracture
10. agriculture
11. acupuncture
12. portraiture
13. denture
14. aperture

Chapter 8 Review

📖 I will read the statements and you will provide the answer.

1. A prefix is a syllable added at the _____ of a word to modify (*change*) its meaning.

2. *Pre* means _____.

3. Name as many prefixes and their meanings that you can recall from memory. You may write them.

4. A dictionary that has been shortened by leaving out or omitting terms or definitions is called an _____ dictionary.

5. A dictionary that includes information such as expanded definitions and language of origin of the words is called an _____ dictionary.

6. Use a _____ to prevent confusion in meanings or awkward spelling, such as reform/re-form and re-enlist/reenlist.

7. Explain how you would read the following word and how you might exaggerate the suffix to spell correctly.
   ☆ agriculture

1. beginning 2. before 3. Prefix answers may vary. 4. abridged 5. unabaridged
6. hyphen 7. Answers may vary.

CONGRATULATIONS!

📖 YOU HAVE COMPLETED
PHONICS STEPS TO READING SUCCESS!

Are you relieved? You now have a shield of reading information to protect you from ignorance. Believe in yourself! Continue to learn more. Achieve great things. Be outstanding in your life's choices and enjoy a piece of the pie of success! Share with others what you have learned.

It does not matter where you come from; it matters where you decide to go.

ACHIEVEMENT AWARD

This award is presented to

_____

for outstanding achievement in

completing Phonics Steps to Reading Success

by Pat Doran, M.Ed.

_____   _____
Signature   Date

It doesn't matter where you come from.

It matters where you decide to go.

APPENDIX

Post Script: After Students Have Been Through Phonics Steps To Reading Success, Then What?

The Next Steps is Teaching the Learner to Using Phonics Concepts to Read with Accuracy and Fluency

PSRS is a skill-building program and not a complete reading program.
As with learning any new skill set, just *knowing* how to decode words is not enough. Students must practice these skills and receive *instructional* feedback when they make errors. Teachers must help students to analyze their errors and to learn from their mistakes so that the students will not make the same mistakes again. All learners should receive much support in their efforts to apply their new knowledge.

Independent reading of decodable text is necessary for every learner to develop accuracy and fluency. The teacher's goal must be for students to read words they encounter, accurately and with automaticity. When students listen to books on tape or listen to someone read as the student follows along, this may develop aural or listening skills, but these are different from reading skills. Moreover, some educational theorists promote a common practice of "echo-reading" or "parrot-reading" by which the teacher reads and the students repeat. While there is value in recitation, we must not confuse it with reading. These are not scientifically proven to be the most effective ways to help learners to gain self-reliant *reading mastery*.

It is true that students *may* benefit somewhat while "reading along" as the teacher models fluent reading. The students *may* gain a *bit* of advantage in repetition and recitation. In addition, cooperation with other students in a small group or learning center projects *may* offer a bit of review options.

However, the focus of instruction must be on teaching each student to gain mastery in the sounding out of new words and the reading of passages accurately, independently, and with fluency. With practice and over time, the student will unconsciously decode words with mastery. To that end, the student will be a self-sufficient, lifelong reader.

Comparing Giving Foundational Phonics Instruction to a New Reader to That of Giving a Teenager Keys to a New Car

In this section, we will examine two very different instructional approaches using driving instruction as an analogy to reading instruction.

Consider a teenage girl who wants to learn to drive. Having her gain access to a car, or even being an observant passenger, is not enough. She will also need to know the laws. Before she actually drives the car, the learner should master basic skills such as the control of the wheel and pedals, the use of the rear-view and side mirrors, as well as how to handle the car in various situations. Then, the student can get into the driver's seat.

With the student in the driver's seat, the instructor supervises and guides her practice as the learner develops good habits. She applies her knowledge in a limited, safe environment. He does not make accommodations or modifications to his requirements simply because she is struggling to apply what he is teaching her. The instructor knows that the difference between her being an excellent driver and a mediocre driver. It can be the difference between life and death.

These habits will be the foundation of all future driving experiences. His guided instruction helps the learner to correct mistakes and to hone skills in a variety of situations, advancing from simple to complex. The goal of the teacher is to instruct and to guide the student, as she becomes a lifelong confident, skilled driver.

In contrast to this effective, direct and explicit instruction with guided practice, let us consider a different instructional strategy. A second driving teacher explains the rules and then says, "Get into the passenger's side. Watch me as I model how to drive on the highway. See how I can go fast and avoid accidents. Notice how I flow in and out of traffic with ease." The teacher pulls the car over. He says, "Here are the keys to the car. Now, that I've modeled for you what good driving is, it is your turn to drive. With practice, you will be just as good as I am."

Obviously, this example is extreme to make a point. With this type of modeled instruction, the student may only assume that "good driving" is going very fast. In this scenario, the student driver is lacking sufficient knowledge and experience. She will hone her driving skills on city streets and highways, modeling her driving after that of her teacher's. However, she may not be aware of any mistakes she is making. This student driver, therefore, also may hone many ineffective or dangerous driving habits. A phrase most drivers have heard or even shouted as some careless driver speeds past is, "Hey, where did you learn to drive?"

Clearly, the two scenarios are at opposite ends of instructional strategies. However, when it comes to reading instruction, we can learn from these two driver's education scenarios.

The role of the instructor is to instill correct habits from the beginning.
All instructors should have as their goal that their students will be knowledgeable, highly skilled, and confident in all academic disciplines. Every student must practice much and independently to be able to apply knowledge with the accuracy and automaticity. When it comes to reading instruction, teachers must be in the instructional and supportive role as they teach. They must merge the "rules of the road" (phonics decoding) with the same kind of "hands-on" guidance that young drivers receive as they practice and develop mastery. Yes, students must become **independent**, **accurate**, and **fluent** readers.

With reading instruction, obviously, there are effective and ineffective methods just as there are with any instructional strategies. For example, some reading programs urge teachers to model their own advanced, fluent reading. Thus, a teacher will read a passage of text, after which their students will repeat what they have heard. Indeed, some students may read along. However, others will recite only what their ears have detected. Still others will pretend to read while hiding their own deficiencies. In a classroom, there is safety in numbers. However, consider what will happen when reading deficiencies carry over into adulthood and the individual must stand alone in a world that relentlessly limits those who cannot read. Unfortunately, this is the experience of millions of adults. It is one that instructors just as relentlessly should aim to prevent.

When the teacher *models* or is the *lead reader* for most reading tasks in class, the student stays in the *passenger seat*, as it were. Regardless of the students' reading abilities, many students may glean the wrong message. Instead of their learning how to read fluently with accuracy, students may internalize a much more basic lesson: "Teacher reads fast." Consequently, students will often attempt to copy the instructor's speed, but not their accuracy.

For that reason, reading instructors should place readers in the *driver's seat*. Students should have countless opportunities to hone their accurate reading and decoding skills independently. They must be able to apply the rules and tools of the phonics code. Much like driving instruction, reading instruction should prepare learners to encounter highly irregular or new situations (words) and not to be surprised or startled by "troublemakers" that they might encounter along the way.

Once students learn the phonics code through PSRS, they will have the skills to decode almost any text. Nevertheless, reading is a skill that requires much practice. The teacher's role in PSRS is to teach, guide, and provide instructional feedback as students--no matter what their ages--make progress.

Reading and Comprehension Strategies

To read and succeed, students *independently* must be able to decode words accurately. Of course, students must increase their **vocabulary** and expand their **background knowledge**. However, once students have completed PSRS, they will be able to decode almost any word in the English language. Frustration and frequent errors will diminish and eventually may disappear. Accuracy, automaticity, and fluency will rise, as will comprehension and self-esteem. Reading will be enjoyable. Vocabulary and knowledge will increase.

Similar to the experience of learning to drive, the knowledge of rules and the practice or repeated application of new skills will be required. Re-reading is a valuable strategy, one that is effective. Consider the following suggested techniques.

READING STRATEGIES FOR ACCURACY AND FLUENCY

✐ STRATEGIES IN A CLASSROOM SETTING: WHOLE CLASS, SMALL GROUPS

Teach the research-proven approach of systematic, synthetic decoding (reading) and encoding (spelling) strategies used in PSRS. Review the concepts as needed. Provide students opportunities to decode and re-read passages independently to develop fluency.

Use only decodable materials for reading texts, tests, or homework. If a student misreads a word in a decodable text, the teacher *as a general practice* should not give the correct word and have the student repeat it. However, the teacher should use this as an opportunity to review concepts, as needed. For example, if a student misreads *use* as *us* by focusing on only the first two letters, the teacher can use this opportunity to have the student review aloud the concept of a vowel team with a consonant blocker and silent e. Refer to page 56.

Foster a positive classroom environment by developing an atmosphere of respect in the classroom. Explain that all students have different skills, talents, and strengths. Explain to the students that every member of the class has different needs and may require varied help and instruction. Everyone learns in different ways and we *all* make mistakes. You may want to share an experience of how you needed someone's help. An appropriate one, for example, would be if you locked yourself out of your car and had to call roadside assistance.

Never permit disrespect in the classroom. Develop mutual respect and have meaningful, simple class mottoes such as the following:
"AT EVERY MOMENT, DO WHAT RESPECT REQUIRES."
"NEVER WASTE A LEARNING MINUTE."

Pre-reading instruction lays the foundation for reading of decodable text and includes an explanation of **vocabulary** and **background knowledge** that is essential for the understanding of what the author wrote. The purpose of reading is to understand what the author intended and not for the readers to construct or to make up their own meanings. Otherwise, students will not grow beyond what they already know.

Authors often assume that the reader has the essential background knowledge of various historical, political, social customs, and the like. They assume that the reader knows something about what is being discussed in the passage or book.

Grammatical concepts must be taught as part of essential background knowledge. They are necessary to aid in the understanding of what authors intend to convey. Grammatical conventions include not only the basics of simple punctuation and capitalization, but also include clauses, dialogue, transitional words and phrases, and complex verb tenses, etc. An instructor may want to consider learning about and teaching sentence diagramming.

Teach an understanding of the vocabulary used in the material.
Discuss and analyze troublemakers **and irregular words** that readers will encounter. Teach a *few highly irregular* words to be recognized *by sight*. Help students to identify the parts of these words that are decodable. Help students to identify the "troublemaker" parts. Provide practice for students to read highly irregular high-frequency *sight* words in decodable context:
 "He **was** hot." "**They** run." "**The** dog sits." "He **does** not run."

Involve all students in the reading aloud. However, there is an exception to this strategy. If a student is new to the class and has not had phonics decoding instruction--or you have not determined his/her decoding mastery—explain that soon the student will be reading with the class. Then, of course, it is up to you, the teacher, to be certain the child learns the essential decoding skills quickly, as soon as possible. Use PSRS as your fast-paced approach for you or a trained volunteer to teach to any new student(s).

The use of small groups can be an effective strategy, but one must use caution. If possible, use similar-ability grouping strategies, not mixed-ability grouping. Avoid embarrassment of weaker students who experience unvoiced, painful humiliation when their peers correct them. Avoid requiring stronger students to squander their in-class time on assignments and activities that are below their level. The grouping of students with similar skill levels provides opportunities for all students to work at developing or improving skills to move to their next level.

All group work must have targeted, specific and measurable academic objectives. There must be individual accountability and an assessment of each of the students to determine if they benefited from the time spent on a group lesson or activity. If the group work is beneficial for all students, find an objective way to measure it. Otherwise, the group work may very well just become time-filling and opportunity-wasting "busywork," or worse.

Generally, it is not good to give individual grades based on the results of the group's work. Frequently, the stronger students will do the bulk of work and the less-cable or less-motivated students will benefit from the work of the others. One high school student was working diligently to earn academic scholarships for college. He complained when his personal grade-point average reflected the many failures of his group's low-quality or incomplete projects. His teacher told him that if he wanted to earn good grades on group projects, it was his job to motivate his peers or to complete the work himself. The student rightfully noted, "Why am I responsible for motivating students when their parents and all of the teachers have not been able to do so?"

Do not use stronger students as "unpaid tutors". Do not lower the reading assignments for stronger readers to accommodate the needs of weaker readers. When the stronger students finish class assignments sooner than some other students, the stronger students must have additional challenging work to do. They must not be used as "unpaid tutors" during regular class hours. It is the teacher's responsibility to help students who need assistance. If any students have completed their work satisfactorily, they should be able to do research, pursue extra-credit assignments, or do other academic reading at or above their level.

Do not lower expectations for weaker readers simply by making *accommodations* that often serve only to impede reading advancement. Do not modify or reduce, as a *general practice*, the amount of required work for these students. Instructors often make accommodations because of the student's lack of skills. For example, the instructor may assign five spelling words instead of ten. This may seem to be a compassionate strategy, *at the time*. However, such accommodations may give students lifelong handicaps as the result of their having had an education that is reduced by one-half. Rather than lowering expectations, the educator must identify the problem and do what is necessary to increase knowledge and to raise the skill level.

Do not assume that the student has been taught correctly in the past. The teacher must assess decoding knowledge, skill-level, as well as accuracy and fluency levels. The teacher must determine what student does not know, and then, find ways to **teach** what is lacking. It can be a disconcerting task.

Do not assume that the publisher's idea of *decodable* is appropriate for your student(s). When something is determined to be *decodable*, it means that authors or publishers assume the students have learned all of the phonics concepts that are required to read the text accurately. It is you, however, who must be the *gatekeeper*. You make the actual decodability determinations that are based on your students' decoding knowledge, mastery, and skills.

Oral reading in a phonics-focused class can be beneficial. Traditionally, reading aloud in class was most effective when all students learned explicit phonics and were capable of reading aloud accurately at grade level. Anyone who had not mastered phonics and was not reading at grade level was not passed on to the next grade. When a student was passed to the next grade, it meant the student was competent enough to do the work at that grade level. In such classrooms, all students had literacy skills to be able accurately to read aloud the academic information in the texts. Oral reading in class was advantageous.

Oral reading in a non-phonics focused class can be detrimental.
All too often, numerous reading levels in a single classroom present teachers with a hodgepodge of problems. This jumbled mess arose when ineffective strategies replaced effective phonics instruction. Even when students were not passed to the next grade, they normally did not benefit by spending yet another year learning ineffective strategies. Thus, when the students did not benefit by repeating the same grade, the practice of social promotion became the *solution*.*

Unfortunately, social promotion often relegates students to an academic sphere of permanent failure or inferiority. Consequently, if ill-prepared students read aloud in class, they may use strategies including guessing and substituting of words. No one can follow along. No one comprehends. The student is disgraced.

Strategies for oral reading in a phonics-focused class: Depending on circumstances, as students are chosen 'round *robin* or in random order, each should read a sentence or paragraph of a <u>decodable</u> material. If the one sentence or paragraph is too brief, extend the student's turn. If the student struggles with the material, the teacher (not another student) may read **softly** through the word or sentence with the student.

---

* To learn more about the history of the teaching of reading and other information about reading instruction, read *The Secret Club: Why and How We Must Teach Phonics and Essential Literacy Skills for Readers of All Ages* by Pat Doran, M.Ed.

Depending on the circumstances, the teacher may use the errors as a "teachable moment" noting that everyone may require help occasionally. The teacher *may* stop the reading to say, "This is a concept with which many of you in class struggle. Let's review this concept before it continues to cause problems for us." Briefly, re-teach and review. Then, thank the students--and especially thank the student who had been reading--for permitting you to interrupt the reading time for this class instruction. The student continues.

Proceed with the students' reading of the sentences or passages. Draw a name randomly to select the next student. Likewise, you may have the next student in the row or group read a sentence or paragraph. However, always take note of which strategies any student will need to have reviewed or re-taught during small group, one-on-one time with teacher, at lunchtime, or after school.

Choral reading of the entire sentence or passage may follow once each student has finished. Do so before proceeding to the next passage.
Be certain all students are reading aloud and not simply "hiding" in the group or pretending to read along.

Comprehension questions should be interspersed throughout the oral reading or the choral reading lesson. At the end of the reading, the teacher must provide a *decodable* practice assignment, *decodable* quiz, or follow-up assessment to be certain that all students can comprehend what they have read.

While students are working on worksheets or assignments, the teacher may walk around, assisting students who may be struggling, frustrated, unsure, or who have questions. If a teacher finds that a student requires help, the teacher may want to indicate the area on the student's paper with a star or a motivational stamp, such as a *happy face*. This will identify for the teacher the specific place where the teacher gave assistance. This technique has two benefits:

1. For the teacher, the indicator serves as code, noting which skill set(s) a student may or may not have mastered and needs to be reviewed.
2. For the student, the location of the star or stamp will seem random, much like the motivational stamps that other students receive.

Caution: When students practice re-reading and/or use rhyming, predictable books, it may appear that they are "reading" the material. In fact, students may be only *reciting* memorized passages. While there is value in recitation, we must not confuse it with reading. Be aware of this potential CAP found in some current reading-curriculum strategies.

FINAL OBSERVATIONS FOR CLASSROOM TEACHERS

HOMEWORK: Homework MUST be decodable to provide practice of *learned* strategies. Parents are expected to *supervise* homework, but not to teach it. Parents may have been taught differently and may not understand what or how you are teaching. Avoid inadvertently creating family conflicts over homework. Parents and teachers must be using the same terminology and strategies.

FAMILY LITERACY NIGHTS: You may consider having Family(or Adult) Literacy Nights during which parents learn the PSRS program. As a result, the parents will know what their children are learning. They will be able to use the same terminology that their children are being taught in your classroom. The parents will be able to reinforce the concepts you are teaching.

An additional benefit is that parents, who may have English language or reading deficiencies themselves, will have increased literacy skills.

NEVER WASTE A LEARNING MINUTE: All students should have three books on or in their desks at all times. These books are to be used when assigned work is completed or during any unassigned time.
1. **Dictionary**
    a. If possible, each student should have a personal paperback dictionary in which each student can highlight the words as they are found or learned.
    b. English language learners must have access to a dual-language dictionary.
2. **A non-fiction book**
3. **A fiction book**

TEACH TO YOUR STUDENT'S FUTURE: While you may not have any influence on the child's home life, you have great opportunities to raise your student's literacy skills. "Teach others how to read and their futures will have no limits." Someone once said, "It doesn't matter where you come from; it matters where YOU decide to go." That is a good motto for you to teach *to* your students.

BECOME AN ANALYTICAL SCHOLAR AND EDUCATOR: You, as an educator, whether inside the classroom or out, must strive to be an analytical scholar. Critique your own work. Accept no excuses. Endeavor to overcome obstacles. Read *all sides* of educational or academic topics to be *fully* informed. Study the educational, scientific research and learn about educators, schools, and programs that are *highly* successful. Emulate what they do. Improve a little each day. Rise above the common, the ordinary.

"It doesn't matter where YOU come from; it matters where YOU decide to go."

Phonics Steps to Reading Success
Basic Rules of Phonics

1. Read and spell from left to right.

2. Be aware of the shape of your mouth as you pronounce sounds.

3. When a vowel in a word stands alone, the vowel says its *short sound* and not its name.

4. Most words with a short vowel sound that end with the /k/ sound are spelled with <u>ck</u> at the end: tack; neck; pick; clock; duck

5. If a word contains any vowel <u>and</u> ends with the letter <u>e</u>, the final <u>e</u> is always silent.

6. If a word ends in <u>le</u>, pronounce /l/ as in bundle; the <u>e</u> is silent and makes no sound.

7. Vowels that appear together are *vowel teams*. Generally, when two vowels are next to each other in a word, the first one says its *name* while the second one is *silent*. Thus, the old saying, "When two vowels go walking, the first one does the talking."

8. In the United States, commonly, the <u>ui</u> is read with an /oo/ sound as in *moon*. The <u>ew</u> is generally pronounced /ēū/ or *long* <u>u</u> the letter <u>w</u>. The <u>w</u> was once a *double u*.

9. When a consonant is between a vowel and its silent, shadow teammate <u>e</u> – as in *ape* or *kite* – the consonant is called a "blocker".
   a. In such a positioning, the first vowel says its name, and the <u>e</u> is silent.
   b. <u>E</u> is the only vowel whose influence can "pass through" the consonant blocker to make the vowel say its name. The <u>e</u> can send its influence through only one consonant blocker, not two.

10. A single e at the end of a word or syllable says its name: when it is the single vowel in an entire word (*he, she*); and when it is the last letter in a single-vowel syllable (*maybe*).

11. When reading unfamiliar words, change the form of your mouth to pronounce each phoneme as it appears in the word.

12. If a word with a vowel ends in y, then the y says /ee/ as in *funny*. Spelling tip: If you hear an /ee/ sound at the end of a word and there is another vowel in the word write y at the end.

13. If a word with a vowel ends in y, the effect of y on the vowel is the same as that of a silent e or, in other words, the vowel is "forced" to say its name. (Two blocker consonants between a vowel and final y keep the vowel short.)

14. If y is the only vowel in a word, it is pronounced as long i as in *my* and *fly*.

15. When o ends a word, the o it says its name as in *go, ego,* and *no*.

16. When y is between consonants, it "acts like" the vowel i. It is either *long* or *short* and pronounced as short /i/ as in *myth* and *gym*. It is pronounced as *long i* in *type* and *cypress*.

17. *Psych* is pronounced /sike/ as in *psychic* and *psychiatry*.

18. AW and AU are pronounced with the mouth shaped like an oval or an egg.

19. When i is followed by a or u, it is not a vowel team. The i is pronounced /ē/ as in *Maria* and *lithium*.

20. The oo vowel digraph has either a long sound as in *moon* or as a short sound as in *foot*.

21. The letter r affects the sound of the vowel that comes before it as in *fur, stir*. However, when a vowel team with a *consonant blocker* (vc-e) occurs, then the first vowel says its name and the final e is silent as in *fire* and *here*.

22. The digraph ch usually is pronounced /ch/ as in *choo-choo* or *chip*. When ch follows a short vowel, a consonant blocker must be present as in *ditch* and *match*.

23. The digraph sh is pronounced /sh/ as in *ship* and *cash*.

24. The digraph th is pronounced /th/ by softly sticking the tongue behind the teeth and blowing out, as in *Thanksgiving* and *bath*.

25. The digraph th can also be pronounced with a "harder" sound, by putting the tongue between the top and bottom teeth, blowing, and vibrating the tongue slightly as in *this, that,* and *those*.

26. The digraph ph is pronounced /f/ as in *phone, dolphin,* and *photo*.

27. The wh can be pronounced hw with a slight puff of air as in *when, whim*. (The w before r is *silent*.)

28. The single vowel i is pronounced as *long i* as in the following exceptions:
    ild as in *wild, mild, child;* ind as in *find, kind, blind;*
    ign as in *sign, design, resign;* igh as in *sigh, high, flight*.

29. In *-igh-* and *-ign- words,* the *g* is silent.

30. The eu and ew teams are pronounced as long u, as in *dew* and *feud*.

31. The diphthongs ow and ou are pronounced as in "Ow! Ouch!" and words, such as *flower, wow, loud,* and *mouth*.

32. Ow can also stand for the *long o* sound as in *snow, show,* and *tow*.
33. The diphthong ou can also stand for the /oo/ sound as in *through*.

34. The diphthong ou also is pronounced as a *short u* when followed by the letter s as in *famous* and *disastrous*.

35. The vowels in alt, alk, aught, all, and ought have the /aw/ sound as in *saw, walk*, and *taught*.

36. The letter c sounds like:
   a. /s/ when followed by e, i, or y as in *center* and *cymbal*;
   b. /k/ when followed by a, o, or u as in *cash*, *coffee*, and *cup*;
   c. /k/ when it is the last letter of a word as in *picnic*.

37. The letter g generally sounds like:
   a. A /j/ when followed by e, i, or y as in *gem* and *gym* (with some exceptions such as *target, girl*);
   b. "Hard g" when followed by a, o, or u as in *gash, go,* and *gush;*
   c. "Hard g when it is the last letter of a word as in *dig* and *dug.*

38. If a ti, ci, or si is followed by a vowel, it makes the /sh/ sound as in *option* and *conscious.*

39. Diphthongs oy and oi are sounded by changing the mouth position first, to pronounce the sound of the first vowel (*long o*) and then, to slide quickly into the sound of the second vowel (*short i*). The result, oi, seems to make one unique phoneme as in *oil* and *toy.*

40. If –ed follows the letters t or d, it is pronounced as /–ted/ or –/ded/.
   a. However, -ed is considered to be a separate syllable as in *plant·ed* and *raid·ed*.
   b. If –ed follows any other letter, it is pronounced simply as /d/ or /t/ as in *harmed* (harmd) or *ripped* (ript) and the –ed is not a separate syllable.

43. The diphthong of qu- usually is pronounced /qw/ as in *queen quest*. It is pronounced infrequently as /k/ in words with a French influence such as: -*quet* as in *croquet;* -*quette* as in *croquette;*-*que* as in *antique.*

44. A troublemaking vowel team is ie. When this team is found in a word, it sometimes breaks the vowel-team rule. Namely, the i is silent and the e says its name, as in *piece.*

Glossary of Selected Terms

Adapted from Webster's New Twentieth Century Dictionary, Unabridged 2nd Edition.

Alphabet   Letters of a specific language in the order fixed by custom. Any system of letters or characters representing sounds. The English Alphabet: *a b c d e f g h I j k l m n o p q r s t u v w x y z*

Consonant   Any speech sound produced by stopping and releasing the air stream (p,t,k,b,d,g), or stopping it at one point while it escapes at another (m, n, l, r), or forcing it through a loosely closed or very narrow passage (f, v, s, zh, sh, z, th, h, w, y), or by a combination of these means (ch, j).

Consonant Phonemes (see Phonemes)
   /b/ **b**at   /c/ **c**at   /d/ **d**og   /f/ **f**ish   /g/ **g**um   /h/ **h**at   /j/ **j**ump   /k/ **k**ite   /l/ **l**ion   /m/ **m**op   /n/ **n**ose   /p/ **p**ig   /q/ (qu) **q**ueen   /ɪ/ **r**at   /s/ **s**ail   /t/ **t**en   /v/ **v**an   /w/ **w**eb   /x/ a**x**   /z/ **z**igzag

Decode   Reading; to translate from a code (letter/symbol) into language (or sound)

Diacritical   Diacritical marks, sign, or point: any mark used with a letter or character to distinguish it from another to indicate how it is pronounced. Examples: ă, ū. Diacritical marks, and so forth, are often explained at the bottom of dictionary pages.

Encode   Spelling; to convert sound into code (letter/symbol)

Phoneme   [Comes from the Greek, *phonema*, meaning a sound.] In linguistics, a class, or family, of closely related speech sounds regarded as a single and represented in phonetic transcription, but the same symbol as the sounds of r in *red, round, bring*: the discernible phonic differences between such sounds are due to the modifying influence of the adjacent sounds.

Phonemic Awareness
   Phonemic awareness is the ability to recognize that a spoken word consists of individual sounds in sequence. The single best predictor of future reading success.

Phonics   1. The method of teaching reading by training beginners to associate the letter(s) with sound values. 2. The science of sound.

Vowel   A voiced speech sound characterized by generalized friction of the air passing in a continuous stream through the pharynx and open mouth, with relatively no narrowing or other obstruction of the speech organs. A letter, as *a, e, i, o,* and *u,* representing such a sound. distinguished from consonant.

Bibliography

BRYANT, MARGARET, Modern English and Its Heritage, The Macmillan Company, New York, 1948, 1962.

CRAWFORD, D.H., Beowolf, Cooper Square Publishers, Inc., New York, 1966.

SABIN, WILLIAM A., The Gregg Reference Manual, Macmillan/McGraw-Hill, New York, 1992.

GROOM, BERNARD, A Short History of English Words, Macmillan & Co., New York, 1962.

MERRIAM-WEBSTER, WEBSTER'S DICTIONARY OF SYNONYMS, G. & C. Merriam Company, Springfield, Massachusetts, 1942.

MILLER, WARDS S., Word Wealth Junior, Holt, Rinehart and Winston, Inc., New York, 1962.

MONROE, MARION AND BERTIE BACKUS, Remedial Reading, Houghton Mifflin Company, New York, 1937.

DORAN, PAT, My Steps Journal: A Character Education Journal, Edu-Steps, Inc. Phoenix, AZ 2014.

PEI, MARIO, The Story of the English Language, J.B. Lippincott Company, New York, 1967.

PYLES, THOMAS, The Origins and Development of the English Language, Harcourt, Brace & World, Inc., New York 1964.

ROBERT, CLYDE, Teacher's Guide to Work Attack, Harcourt, Brace & World, Inc., New York 1956.

READER'S DIGEST, Complete Wordfinder, The Reader's Digest Association, Inc., Pleasantville, New York, 1996.

TAYLOR, ALBERT, JOHN C. GILMARTIN, WILLIAM A. BOYLAN, Correct Spelling with Dictionary Study/ 5th Year, Noble & Noble, Publishers, Inc., New York, New York, 1941.

WEBSTER'S NEW TWENTIETH CENTURY DICTIONARY, 2nd Edition with Outline History of the English Language, unknown publication information.

WOOD, CLEMENT, The Complete Rhyming Dictionary and Poet's Craft Book, Garden City Books, Garden City, New York, 1936.

SPECIAL ACKNOWLEDGEMENT
To George O. Cureton and Jeannie Eller, www.actionreading.com

INDEX

SUBJECT	PAGE
ab, prefix meaning *from*	152
accents	47, 66
See dialects	
ad, prefix meaning *to*	153
ae vowel team	55
ai vowel team	50
al, all	113
ante-, prefix meaning **before**	154
anti-, prefix meaning **against**	154
ar	82
au	78, 80, 111, 12, 113
aw	77, 80
ay	48
bi (prefix meaning *two*)	101
c, /k/ sound,	
followed by any letter other than e, i, y	119, 122
c, /s/ sound, followed by e, i, y	117, 118
c-words Test	120
c-words Test Answers	121
cc-, double *c*	122
ch (also –tch)	92, 93, 94, 95
-cial	130, 132
-cient	132
-cious	130
circum (prefix meaning **around**)	155
-ck	28
-ck word practice/game	30
-ck words, spelling	29
comprehension	26, 34, 35
Certificate of Completion	175
con, prefix meaning **with, bring together**	156

192

Consonant blockers	56
Consonant blockers practice	57
context clues	34, 35
contra, prefix meaning against	157
de, prefix meaning down, from, reverse action	157
-dge	95
dis	158
Dialects	47, 66
Dictionary	
abridged	151
unabridged	151
Digraphs	
ch	92, 93, 95
ck	28
ph	98
th	26, 97
Explanation of	91
Diphthongs	
oi, oy	136
ue	106
dis (prefix meaning *apart*)	158
Dyslexia (symptoms)	31, 32
e, final e with no other vowel	56
ea troublemakers	47, 70, 71
ea vowel team	43, 44
ee vowel team	52
-ed	139-140
ELL (English Language Learners)	68
er	85
Errors,	
Reading	31, 32
Spelling	31
eu	107
ew (u-sounding vowel team)	53, 106
em- (prefix)	159
ex- (prefix)	159

g
    followed by any letter other than e, i, y   124
    g-word test   126
    g-word test answers   127
    ge   125, 126
    gh   111, 112
    gi   125-126
    gn (words beginning with)   128

gy   125-126

History
    Alphabet, early development of   90
    Chaucer's Canterbury Tales   144
    English (blend of many languages)   84
    eu, ew   107
    Franklin, Benjamin   46
    g (sound/spelling variations)   124
    Great Vowel Shift   45
    igh, ind, ild   102

    Latin   145
    Origins of words
        Old Spellings   72
    ph   98
    Roots of the English Language   67, 84, 144

    Sight Words   69
        ph(origin of)   98
    sh (origin of)   96
    sh (sound/spelling variations)
        -sier, zier   129
        -sion   129
        -sure, zure   129
    Spelling adaptations   124
    th (origin of)   97
    wh (origin of)   99

    Webster, Noah   46

    i before *e* except after *c*   147
    ***ie* breaks the rules**   148
    ***ie* vowel team**   51

igh	112
il (prefix meaning *not* (See also prefixes in, im, ir)	160
ild	102
in (prefix meaning *not* (See also prefixes il, im, ir)	160
in prefix meaning *in, put in*	159
ind	102
ing	128, 139
inter (prefix meaning *between, among*)	161
intra (prefix meaning *within*)	161
intro/intra-, prefix meaning *within*	161
ir **words**	86
ir (prefix meaning *not* (See also prefixes il, im, ir)	160
-*le* at the end	33
Left to Right, *Reading from*	16, 18, 19, 20, 27
Long Vowel Story	38-42
Long vowel teams	
ae	55
ai	50
ay	48
ea	14, 70
ie	51
ee	52
oa	49
oe	54
ue, ui (See also *ew)*	53, 106
-with consonant blockers	56
mis (prefix meaning *wrong*)	162
names (long, silly)	108
-ng, words with *ang, ing, ong, ung*	128
nonsense words	19, 20, 29, 34, 35, 60, 104
oa vowel team	49
oe vowel team	54
oi (see also, *oy*)	136
oo	81

or	83
ou	109, 110, 111, 112
ous	109
ow	109, 110
oy (see also, oi))	136
p (silent)	107
per (prefix meaning *through*)	163
ph	98
Poster	
Read Left to Right	27
post- (prefix meaning *after*)	164
pre (prefix meaning *before*)	
prefixes (review of)	
other	171
pro (prefix meaning *for, before*)	165
psych	146
qu	142, 143
"R-controlled" **vowels**	
ar	82
er	85
ir	86
or	83
Reading errors	32
Re (prefix meaning **again, back**)	166
Reviews	
Chapter 1	21
Chapter 2	36
Chapter 3	62
Chapter 4	88
Chapter 5	100
Chapter 6	115
Chapter 7	149
Chapter 8	173
Rules	
Reading	19
Spelling	20

Schwa e	46, 52
*se (*prefix meaning **aside, apart**)	167
sh diagraph	46
-sial	130
-sion	130
-sient	132
Sight Words (about)	
Problems with	31, 32
Memorization	69
Practicing (sight-words used in sentences)	69, 70
(See History)	
-sion, -tion, **Teams**	130
***Sub* (**prefix meaning *above*)	167
super- prefix meaning *above*	168
Spelling	
Adaptations (See History)	124
Basic rule for	20
-ch, -tch, dge, wr words	95
Errors	31
How to study words for spelling accuracy	61
Inventive	73
Rule: i before e except after e	147
s with the /zh/ sound	129
Troublemakers Spelling Tips	74, 75
Standard American English	67
English Language Learners	68
Suffix	53
-able/-ible	32
-ted/-ded	139, 140
-ing	139
-ture	172
Syllables	
Rules	133-134
Dictionaries (as denoted in)	78
-tch	93, 94, 95

-ted/-ded	139, 140
-th	97
-tial	130
-tient	132
-tion	130, 131
-tious	130
trans (prefix meaning across, through, beyond)	168
tri (**prefix meaning** *three*)	169
-ture	172

Troublemakers
    ea   70
    ia, iu   79

Vowels (also see specific vowels)

e, final e with no other vowel	56
long vowel sounds with team talkers	43, 44
short	24
Team-Talker Story	38-42
ue **vowel team**	106
ui **vowel team**	53, 106
un (prefix meaning *not*	169
uni (prefix meaning *1*)	169
ur	87

Vowel Teams

with consonant blocker	57
ia troublemaker	79
iu troublemaker	79
wh	99
words, nonsense	19, 20, 29, 34, 35, 60, 104
wr	95
-y as a vowel	64, 65, 146
-y as final letter in words with other vowels	64
-y as at the end of words without vowels	65
-y- as within words, between consonants	146

EDU-STEPS, INC.

From the Author and Staff at Edu-Steps, Inc.

Dear Reader,

We are pleased to hear from the teachers, parents, and self-learners who say that they enjoy using the materials from Edu-Steps, Inc.

If you have a suggestion, a comment, a question, or a testimony about your successes, please feel free to contact us at www.edu-steps.com. We look forward to hearing from you. Also, if you find this program helpful, please tell others about it. It is available in various media formats.

If you send us a testimony and permit us to use it on our website and in our advertising materials, please add a note saying that you give us your permission. We will be pleased to use your name or keep your comments anonymous.

Thank you,

Pat Doran, M.Ed. and Staff

Our products:

- **Pat Doran's PHONICS STEPS TO READING SUCCESS: A FAST-PACED, WORD-ATTACK SYSTEM FOR DEVELOPING AND IMPROVING READING SKILLS, 5th Edition** (Spiral bound, full-color, 8 1/2" X 11")

- **Pat Doran's PHONICS STEPS TO READING SUCCESS: A FAST-PACED, WORD-ATTACK SYSTEM FOR DEVELOPING AND IMPROVING READING SKILLS, 5th Edition** (Unabridged, convenient, compact paperback format, black and white, , 6" X 8")

- **Study cards (flash cards) for PHONICS STEPS TO READING SUCCESS: A FAST-PACED, WORD-ATTACK SYSTEM FOR DEVELOPING AND IMPROVING READING SKILLS, 5th Edition** (Classroom-sized, spiral-bound, full-color, 8 1/2" X 11")

- **Study cards (flash cards) for PHONICS STEPS TO READING SUCCESS: A FAST-PACED, WORD-ATTACK SYSTEM FOR DEVELOPING AND IMPROVING READING SKILLS, 5th Edition (For individuals** or learning-center activities, approx. 4" X 5")

- **Pat Doran's GRAMMAR STEPS FOR SPEAKING AND WRITING SUCCESS** (Lessons and practice)

- **MY STEPS JOURNAL: BUILDING CHARACTER ONE STEP AT A TIME** by Pat Doran, M.Ed. and Valerie Plancarte

For information about professional development seminars, to learn about other products or to contact Edu-Steps, please visit www.edu-steps.com.